I0592439

Not a Simple Story

Not a Simple Story

Love and Politics in a Modern Hebrew Novel

Sharon Green

LEXINGTON BOOKS
Lanham • Boulder • New York • Oxford

LEXINGTON BOOKS

Published in the United States of America
by Lexington Books
4720 Boston Way, Lanham, Maryland 20706

P.O. Box 317
Oxford OX2 9RU, UK

Copyright © 2001 by Lexington Books
First paperback edition published 2002

All rights reserved. No part of this publication may be reproduced,
stored in a retrieval system, or transmitted in any form or by any
means, electronic, mechanical, photocopying, recording, or otherwise,
without the prior permission of the publisher.

British Library Cataloguing in Publication Information Available

The hardcover edition of this book was previously catalogued by the Library of Congress
as follows:
Green, Sharon M., 1954–
    Not a simple story   love and politics in a modern Hebrew novel / Sharon M. Green.
        p.   cm.
    Includes bibliographical references and index.
    1. Agnon, Shmuel Yosef, 1888–1970—Criticism and interpretation. 2. Agnon,
Shmuel Yosef, 1888–1970. Sipur pashut. 3. Love in literature. I. Title.

PJ5053.A4 Z59845   2001
892.4'35—dc21   2001042731

ISBN 978-0-7391-0474-3

Printed in the United States of America

♾™ The paper used in this publication meets the minimum requirements of American
National Standard for Information Sciences—Permanence of Paper for Printed Library
Materials, ANSI/NISO Z39.48–1992.

To my husband Ken
and our children Alexander, Daniel, and Jonathan
—with love

Contents

Preface

The Hebrew novelist Shmuel Yosef Agnon (1887-1970) has been an enigma to literary scholars and critics for almost a century. Though awarded the Nobel Prize for literature in 1966 and hailed as a "modern Hebrew classic" by Gershom Scholem, Agnon is nevertheless a writer whose work remains shrouded in mystery. This is partly to do with the fact that Agnon himself is a writer who speaks with two voices—that of the pious storyteller, and that of the secular modernist—both of which seem to assert equal authority in his work. The question is: who is the true Agnon? Is it possible to understand his work without solving this fundamental dilemma?

Although an author might never choose to disclose his whole self to his readers, there is generally one work within a writer's oeuvre that reveals more about himself than any other. Agnon wrote such a work in 1935, the novel *A Simple Story*, an ironic tale about star-crossed lovers in a Jewish town in eastern Europe. It is a seminal work, not because it parallels the facts of Agnon's biography (to the contrary), but rather because more than any other of his novels, it presents a piercing vision of Agnon's *ideas*: his approach to society, human frailty, religion, politics, and, most of all, to romantic love, the unavailability of which pervades nearly all of his works.

Understanding Agnon's ideas, however, is no simple task, partly because of the depth and breadth of his own knowledge of literature, psychology, myth, and religion. A clear case is the novel *A Simple Story*, whose ideas are difficult for us to understand fully unless we recognize that its essential form derives from the classic love tale commonly found in European literature. Yet, at the same time, Agnon's love tale is a distinctly *Jewish* one, in which the social, religious, and political conditions of Jewish existence play a key role in determining the tragic outcome. Indeed, it becomes increasingly clear that the Jewish aspect *is* the problem, and what started out as a pristine love story, modeled on the European prototype, becomes a grotesque version of everything that it initially promised to be.

Is Agnon therefore suggesting that Jewish society prevents the individual Jew from achieving happiness? Is he even implying that the untenable condition of European Jewry as a whole is reflected in this truncated tale of frustrated love? If Agnon is to be properly understood, it is essential to find the connection in his writing between the individual and the society, between the personal and the political. It is indeed conceivable that Agnon, writing in 1935 about the naive love of a vulnerable youth, was also writing about the illusory hopes of a defenseless people. This is not to say that Agnon was writing a purely allegorical tale about the disfigured and precarious condition of European Jewry. It is merely to suggest that if the enigma of Agnon's work is to be deciphered, it will only be by understanding him as a *thinker* whose thoughts run deeper than the "simple story" that he tells. It should also confirm that in the case of Agnon, the artist and the thinker are in no way incompatible, but are part of a whole that makes for the highest form of fiction.

Acknowledgments

There are many people and institutions to thank for helping me to prepare this study at the various stages of its formulation and completion. First of all, I would like to thank the various foundations that provided financial support for my research and writing: the Social Sciences and Humanities Research Council of Canada; the American Association of University Women; the Memorial Foundation for Jewish Culture; and the University of Toronto, for the Ray D. Wolfe Fellowship.

At the earliest stages of writing this book, three of my teachers gave me invaluable encouragement, for which I am truly grateful: Professors Marvin Fox, Naftali Chaim Brandwein, and Joshua Rothenberg, all of Brandeis University. Although all three of them are now departed from this world, I would like to acknowledge their wise instruction and, above all, their *mentschlichkeit*, attributes I shall always associate with their names.

I would also like to extend my warm thanks to Professor Yehuda Friedlander of Bar-Ilan University, who read my work with care and whose suggestions helped me to hone my thinking and writing. I am truly indebted to him for sharing his vast knowledge with me and for enthusiastically supporting my attempt to take an independent stand on many issues raised in the book.

In addition, I would like to thank a number of friends who actively encouraged me to get this book published: Ellen Birnbaum, Arthur Fish, Donna Orwin, Judy Shier, and Martin Yaffe.

A very personal thank-you goes to my three children, Alexander, Daniel, and Jonathan. Although it is surely difficult to write a book with children underfoot, it is a testimony to their sweet temperaments that it was possible to do it nonetheless. I hope I can bring them as much pride as they bring me.

Of course my deepest thanks go to my husband Ken, who is also my dearest friend. He did countless readings and rereadings of the chapters, helping to pull me through the rough spots and rejoice over the breakthroughs. He even befriended Agnon almost as much as I. Words hardly suffice to express my indebtedness to him—for his constancy, intelligence, good humor, and love. Half the satisfaction of finishing this work is sharing it with him.

Chapter 1

The Problem of Love
in Modern Literature:
A Historical Overview

Romantic love, one of the fundamental human realities, is constantly explored in the novels and short stories of Shmuel Yosef Agnon. The love between a man and a woman is in fact at the very center of some of Agnon's most fully developed works.[1] Indeed, there is an entire series of stories by Agnon that can be categorized simply as "love stories." One novel in particular stands out as the closest thing to the classic love novel that Agnon produced. This is the work modestly entitled *Sipur pashut* (*A Simple Story*), written in 1935.[2]

It is not surprising that this novel that focuses on love is also considered by many critics to be the work by Agnon most akin to the Western novel.[3] This would seem to be because the novel as a form in Western literature is so closely tied to the idea of romance. And romantic love, in its traditional manifestation,[4] is at the core of the plot structure of the classic Western novel.[5]

Love, however, consistently takes a course in Agnon's work that, on the surface, seems closer to his twentieth-century contemporaries than it is to the Western classics. That is, love inevitably fails in Agnon's world, and the romantic attractions, encounters, and vows between men and women become hopelessly defeated.

The consistency of this tragic outcome leads one to ask the question: *why* does love fail in Agnon's works? Can it merely be explained as a product of the cynicism, malaise, and rejection of traditional forms characteristic of the twentieth-century writer?[6] Can Agnon simply be fit into the category of modern nihilist or existentialist alongside the likes of Dostoyevsky, Joyce, Kafka, and Sartre?[7] True, Agnon's work often possesses elements that are recognizably part of modernist conventions: symbolic dreams, ambiguous endings, interior monologue, and complex psychological portraits. In fact, there would seem to be much legitimacy in claiming Agnon as a thoroughly modern European writer who can take his place among these modernists with little qualification.

This simplistic categorization, however, falls short in several respects, most particularly because it makes it impossible to explain the numerous "antimodern" complexities of Agnon's works. In fact, one would be forced to bend Agnon out of shape in order to fit him neatly into such a scheme. Indeed, one would have to virtually obscure the fact that he chose to write in an "archaic," non-Western language, that was also generally nonspoken. Similarly, one would have to ignore the fact that he wrote in a style that was far closer to the meandering voice of an ancient storyteller than to the minimalist prose of the alienated individual.

Thus, it would seem that the consistent failure of love in the works of Agnon cannot be explained only as the result of the cynicism of the modernist, since there are too many contradictory aspects to his work that defy such a simple categorization. In fact, it is my contention that if we view Agnon not as a European modernist, but as a *Hebrew* modernist (a term with its own oxymoronic implications),[8] composing his works in a traditional Jewish language and almost exclusively about Jewish society, we may be better equipped to understand the indigenous reasons why love is portrayed in such a tragic light. In other words, the failure of love can be explained as the result of a series of complex factors at work that present conflicting demands upon the modern Hebrew writer who is bound to the modern period, yet who continuously reaches before and beyond it.

What are the specific conflicts that would besiege a writer like Agnon, and compel him to constantly fashion an imaginative universe where love cannot flourish? It is my view that there are four distinct conflicts that plagued the Hebrew writer[9] and that together account for the failure of love in his fiction.

First, the modern Hebrew writer was faced with a sociological conundrum of considerable weight. That is, his very identity as a *Hebrew* writer implied a connection with traditional Judaism, but at the same time this meant a tie to a living civilization character- ized by a strict social hierarchy with fixed laws, institutions, and mores. However much he desired the modern transformation of these structures, he was also paradoxically faced with the fact that the very continuity of this civilization was threatened by the forces of modernity which he as a *modernist* (by the very nature of his profession as a writer) could not help but promote.

Second, if the writer was to maintain his identity as a Hebrew writer, the weight of Jewish history could hardly be far from his consciousness. But this history also provided the Hebrew writer with contradictions to bear. His historical memory would naturally contain numerous scenes of persecutions and expulsions; yet stretching back further, it would also proudly recall the memory of an ancient noble past and the promise of its restoration. Wherein lay the identity of the modern Hebrew writer—in the suffering of recent history or in the nobility of ancient lore?

Third, the Hebrew writer was challenged by the specific psy- chological makeup of his Jewish character types. One could even say that there may in fact be psychological phenomena that mani- fest themselves uniquely in the Jewish personality. For example, is the Jewish psyche (for a complex of reasons) more prone to guilt complexes, obsessive behavior, masochistic impulses, etc.? If this is so, it could, on the one hand, limit the possibility of creating "normal" plots; on the other hand, these psychological phenomena could lead to an exploration of new directions in plot which would set Hebrew writing apart from other literatures in a decisive way.

Fourth, a writer such as Agnon who emerged from a deeply re- ligious environment could not help but be conflicted by theological issues no matter how modern a position on religion he held. From this vantage point, it would be difficult for him to avoid facing the restless shifting of his contemporaries who have abandoned traditional religion even as they choose other forms of self-dedication offered by the modern world. Does the abandonment of religion truly free the spirit from harmful constraints and clear a path for new opportunities of achieving happiness? Or, does the loss of religion entail a loss of other things which can never be replaced or substituted?

It is a testimony to the fact that Agnon was taken up with such indigenous Jewish concerns that he generally chose to write in a style that more closely resembles the Jewish midrashic texts than the modern Western novel. As we mentioned previously, however, one of Agnon's shorter novels, *Sipur pashut*, defies this usual style and to a high degree bears a striking resemblance to the modern Western love novel, not only in terms of narrative style but also in regard to plot, characterization, and thematic device. In fact, I would go so far as to say that the novel *Sipur pashut* should be rightly seen as Agnon's paradigmatic work on love, with all of his love stories variations on it.[10]

But before examining how Agnon imitates (and ultimately undermines) this classic form, it is first requisite to ask what constitutes a classic love story and what are its typical features in Western literature. And since the theme of our study is that of love and the question of why it is a problem rather than a solution in Agnon's fictional world, we will also briefly review historically how other writers have utilized the elements of the classic love tale in order to convey their particular message. In this way, it may be possible to judge more clearly if Agnon can indeed be placed in the historical spectrum of writers who have taken up this theme and presented it anew.

The Evolution of the Love Story

Although there is no clear consensus among literary historians about the exact origins of the classic love story, most generally follow Northrop Frye who traces its roots back to the Greeks, specifically to Greek New Comedy.[11] One could also argue that the Bible presents patterns of courtship and love that are not unlike their Greek counterparts. In *The Art of Biblical Narrative*,[12] Robert Alter devotes an entire chapter to the pattern of betrothal in the

Bible and outlines a structure (particularly evident in the story of Jacob and Rachel) that appears to be strikingly similar to the structure of love stories seen in later centuries throughout Western literature. Perhaps literary theorists Robert Scholes and Robert Kellogg sum it up best by saying that it is so basic a story pattern that we can trace it back to the earliest rituals of man. They state that "in pure romance we can see a refined and displaced aspect of fertility ritual."[13]

It may seem that we need hardly describe the features of the classic love tale, it being so familiar a form that its patterns are discernible even within genres as diverse as the ancient myth, the *Bildungsroman*, and the modern potboiler. Nonetheless, it is of primary importance to isolate the separate components of the love story in order to clearly distinguish which of its parts are essential to its character and which are malleable aspects of its time and context.

The plot structure of the classic love story can be described quite succinctly: boy and girl fall in love; a vow of affection is exchanged; an interference of some sort (usually parental) comes between them and separates the lovers; the separation is overcome and the lovers are reunited (in comedy), or the lovers are not reunited causing one or both to die at the end (in tragedy).

Interestingly, one of the purest examples of the classic love story is also one of the best known, and this is the story of Cinderella.[14] Handed down through the generations as a fairy tale for children, this archetypal story distils in pristine fashion all of the elements of the classic love story that recur in countless other stories of a more sophisticated nature.[15] A close look at the Cinderella story in fact reveals many other conventions of the genre beyond the bare skeleton of the plot structure sketched out above.

The first crucial detail of the Cinderella story is perhaps also the most determinative of the story as a whole, and this is the revelation that Cinderella is an orphan. The fact that the heroine (or in some stories the hero) possesses no parents, and thus no protectors, makes her particularly vulnerable and exposed to harm. This state alone makes her immediately worthy of the reader's sympathy and concern. Moreover, along with being orphaned is the accompanying plight of being poor. In the case of Cinderella, the loss of her father leaves her both emotionally and economically bereft, for she becomes the helpless victim of a cruel and greedy stepmother who steals Cinderella's rightful inheritance and reduces her to a lowly servant.

Examples of other such orphans who are set adrift into the world, and who become easy prey to scoundrels and deceivers, are so numerous in modern literature that we need mention only a few to make the point: Pamela in Richardson's *Pamela*; Jane in Charlotte Bronte's *Jane Eyre*; David in Dickens's *David Copperfield*; and even Fanny in Jane Austen's *Mansfield Park*.[16]

The fact that the mistreated or victimized orphan always falls in love with someone above her station is a standard feature of this genre. But let us not hastily conclude that this merely serves the purpose of satisfying the reader's taste for the unlikely or the miraculous. It serves another purpose as well. The person with whom the orphan falls in love plays a crucial role in the dramatic action by serving as a liberator who frees the orphan from her bondage and who provides the needed path of escape from her plight. And this is the way it must be. If the lover were merely another waif sharing the orphan's lowly station, then surely all hope of the orphan ever escaping her plight would be dubious. Within the bounds of conventional society, the pair of downtrodden lovers would simply sink together into a sea of drowned hopes. In other words, without adequate wealth and social standing, the pair would never possess the power to overturn the injustice of the orphan's mistreatment. Thus, the ideal object of the orphan's love is often he with the *most* power in the land, i.e., those of royal birth, as in the case of Cinderella's prince. Failing this, what is needed to rescue the orphan from her plight is a character who at least approximates all of the "princely virtues"—aristocratic breeding, fine sensibility, moral integrity, and money. This is true for characters as diverse as Edmund in *Mansfield Park*, Mr. B. in *Pamela* (after he learns his lesson), and Daniel in George Eliot's *Daniel Deronda* (despite his Jewish origins).

The genre also possesses conventions determining the way in which the lovers first express their feelings for one another and this typically takes place in the form of a vow or a pledge. This is a crucial turning point in the plot because it is from then on that the reader's expectations are firmly set that the lovers *must* be united, despite the unequal and therefore problematic nature of their circumstances. The vow itself (surely a foretaste of their future marriage vows) sometimes takes on various forms. In some works, the vow is an open and clearly spoken pledge of undying affection (as in some versions of the Cinderella story), and in other stories it is no more than an exchanged look, touch, or word. At times, the lovers even deny to themselves what has transpired between them, but the reader is supplied with enough information by the author that he knows that a powerful event has taken place, and that henceforth these two lovers are meant to be together. There are some works in which the utter necessity of the lovers' union takes on an almost mystical air. In such cases, the vow becomes almost a sacred pledge which, if broken, could have disastrous consequences.[17] But even in the most prosaic love story, the vow is always the pivotal act upon which the outcome of the plot depends: if the vow is kept, then the story ends happily; if the vow is broken, then the story ends tragically.

The final union of the two lovers is never achieved without a struggle to overcome some obstacle, perhaps conveying that the effort to gain something of value rarely comes easily. Usually, the main obstacle is presented by a character who interferes in some way with the lovers' union. In the Cinderella story, it is the wicked stepmother who plays this role by trying to keep Cinderella home from the palace ball, somehow knowing that if the prince should meet Cinderella then it would be she whom he would choose to be his wife. But it does not always have to be a stepmother who is the interferer in such stories (though the stepmother is perhaps the most archetypal model). Nonetheless, it is a role generally given to a parental figure, oftentimes the father of the lover with wealth and social standing who is outraged that his offspring intends to break with convention and marry one beneath his station. At this point, the struggle of the lovers to overcome this interference takes on an added function: their struggle becomes as much about loosening rigid social conventions as it is about fulfilling the desires of two individuals who have pledged their troth.[18] Although in some works, the interferer is no more than a benignly vexatious character (more of a busybody than a villain), in other works the interfering party exhibits distinctly sinister qualities. In this type of story, the struggle by the lovers to overcome the interference of such a villain in order to be finally united suggests something of a larger-scale "war" of good versus evil. If the lovers succeed, it is not merely a personal victory, but also the highly satisfying triumph of all that is good and just winning out over evil and injustice.

The final stage of the classic love story involves the particular *method* that is undertaken to overcome or "defeat" the obstacle blocking the union of the lovers. In tragedies, of course, this is never achieved, though the standard tragic ending usually makes the point that the lovers will nevertheless be united after their death, despite the fact that they were unable to overcome the obstacle blocking their love in their lifetime (as in "Tristan and Iseult," "Heloise and Abelard," etc.).[19] But in the comedic mode, the obstacle that seemed insurmountable is eventually conquered, and the lovers gracefully unite and "live happily ever after." The question is, *how* is the unwieldy obstacle overthrown?

In the story of Cinderella, it seems at first glance that it is the presence of the fairy godmother that would prove to be the means by which the lovers would finally become united. After all, she is the character who intervenes in the middle of the story and magically furnishes Cinderella with all the finery necessary to go to the royal ball in order to meet the prince. She also is the one who provides Cinderella with the treasured glass slippers, the only clue the prince later possesses to help him find his lost love. But even in this simple fairy tale, it is actually nothing wondrous or magical in nature that serves to overcome the obstacle in the lovers' path and bring their love to fruition. This is because it is neither the fairy godmother nor the glass slipper that truly unites the prince with Cinderella. Rather, it is the prince's firm determination and unbending faith that he would find Cinderella which accomplishes more than any supernatural intervention.

And yet, there is something additional that brings the story to its happy conclusion, perhaps even more important than the prince's resolute determination and faith. This is what we might call the "democratic spirit" at work in these classic stories.[20] In the Cinderella story, the prince seeks his beloved one in the highest *and* lowest places after she disappears from the ball at the stroke of midnight, making way for the possibility that it could turn out to be the poorest or simplest maiden who will fit the glass slipper and reveal herself to be the missing lady. And indeed this is the case. When the prince discovers that the slipper fits the lowly maid dressed in rags and covered in cinders, he sees beyond the outer form and recognizes her as the beloved one he has been seeking. And just as her rags and cinders are ignored, so is her lack of wealth and social standing meaningless to him. He takes her for his bride and raises her up to be his princess.

Does this mean, then, that grand endings such as this are actually conveying that every person potentially merits such a lofty elevation as does Cinderella? The answer would have to be no. These stories show that there are certain individuals who are so exceptional that they merit being raised to a noble status. Therefore, although we may call such stories "democratic" in spirit, the emphasis in these stories on crossing the lines between rich and poor, or nobleman and commoner, cannot be equated with egalitarianism. Rather, such stories depict a struggle only on behalf of those who are deemed exceptionally deserving, whether due to great beauty, intelligence, talent, or goodness.

It was within these parameters that the writers of the Neoclassical period of modern literature[21] transformed and perfected the art of the love story. Their ideas surely reached their highest expression and refinement in the novels of Jane Austen, even though her work is not always considered part of the Neoclassical period *per se*. In Jane Austen's novels, the obstacles in the path of true love can always be overcome, but not because of the superiority of anyone's "outer qualities" such as beauty and grace, as is the stuff of fairy tales. Though not denigrating the importance of the "outer" self, Jane Austen stressed the cultivation of the "inner" self as the most vital task, or what might be better termed the "building of character," both moral and intellectual.

In Jane Austen's *Pride and Prejudice*, the heroine Elizabeth Bennet is of a definitively lower social and economic class than her aristocratic admirer Mr. Darcy, but she is nevertheless his perfect match in terms of wit, judgment, and most importantly moral refinement. The true obstacle blocking their union is not money or social opinion (though these are indeed hindrances presented by

Darcy's imperious aunt, Lady Catherine De Bourgh); rather, the real problem is an internal "blockage" on the part of the lovers themselves. Both Elizabeth and Darcy suffer from pride and prejudice, character flaws which must be recognized and overcome before either can submit to a free and unbiased love for the other.

Hence, the emphasis on nobility of *character* rather than nobility of birth, which is merely hinted at in fairy stories such as Cinderella, is brought into sharp focus by authors in the Neoclassical period such as Jane Austen who, as we have seen, judges individual merit more on "internal" qualities. But note that an additional factor can be detected in such works. Not only those of "lower" birth are required to display their virtues (in order to be raised in status), but those of "higher" birth are also put to the test. The latter must prove themselves worthy of the station to which they have been born, not only as an act of legitimating their social rank but as a means of attaining the love of a partner they must merit by reason of "character." Therefore, the ideal love of this period occurs when both partners prove themselves to be spiritual equals despite the inequality of their birth. Only then can they both live as deserving leaders and examples to their society, truly meriting the higher social plane in which they have been granted a cherished place.

Now that the features of the archetypal romance have been outlined, the culmination of such form reaching its peak in the Neoclassical period of modern literature, we can proceed to explore how the boundaries of this genre were strained by the Romantics and the Realists in the nineteenth century, and then how its conventions were virtually overturned by the Modernists in the late nineteenth and twentieth centuries. The relatively tame humanism of the Neoclassical period, with its belief in the ability of man's reason to sublimate the passions (tempered by due skepticism about its universal application) opened the floodgates to a more radical faith in man. The Romantics[22] took up the cause of humanism where the Neoclassical writers left off, casting aside the skepticism and increasing the optimism. But it was a new "human" who was so heartily embraced by the Romantics. To them, it was not the passions that were the threat to human happiness, but it was society that was to blame. Man was essentially good, and the truly "authentic" human being was the "natural" man who was free to experience the depths of his emotions unshackled by the harmful constraints of civilized society. The goal was to alter society sufficiently so that man's innate capacity for goodness could be allowed to flourish.[23]

Therefore, the faith in man inherent in the Neoclassical period burst into full flower in the Romantic era, celebrating man's seemingly limitless capacity for deep feeling. This indeed served to expand the love story's possibilities in several areas. In particular, this era brought with it a whole new focus on classes of society and types of characters which hitherto had been ignored. For example, in their search for the "natural" man, writers were now portraying the life of the lower classes and simple folk as possessing intrinsic interest and value. As well, the uncommon and the unusual became standard literary subjects: portraits of abandoned children, exotic strangers, underworld gangs, and even mentally deranged individuals all found their way into these works.[24] Writers were also attempting to capture extremes of emotion—from the heights of passion and exaltation to the depths of melancholy, cunning, and cruelty.[25]

But despite the new directions in social setting and character typology displayed in these literary works, the love stories written at this time remained relatively unchanged in terms of their basic structure and components. Jane Eyre, the poor orphan of Charlotte Bronte's creation, still gets her rich Mr. Rochester—granted, only after his mad wife who is locked in the attic burns down the manor with herself inside! Likewise, Victor Hugo's orphaned Cosette in *Les Miserables* ends up with her aristocratic, revolution-seeking Marius, despite the scourge of suffering and death preceding their union. In other words, orphans and aristocrats, vows and obstacles, still remained the set ingredients of the romantic stew. True, emotion had become more blatant, and setting had become more exotic, but the basic plot structure remained generally intact.

At the same time, the love story did undergo some severe stresses and strains in the Romantic era. Perhaps the most significant factor challenging the conventions of the classic love story was in the realm of characterization. This was particularly evident in the *type* of character now given the role as orphan. No longer is it an earnest middle class lady or a virtuous young house maid who earns the right to a noble destiny. For example, Emily Bronte allows the volatile street waif Heathcliff to take the orphan's role in *Wuthering Heights*; George Eliot introduces an exotic young Jewess to play this part in *Daniel Deronda*; writers as diverse as Flaubert, Dostoyevsky, Balzac, and Dumas go so far as to let prostitutes fill the role.[26] In the Neoclassical period of modern literature, such characters were rarely portrayed even in passing, not to mention promoted to the role of romantic lead. Now with the Romantics, such "undesirables" were beginning to take center stage, claiming the right to aim for higher realms—and sometimes winning it, too, by means of the love union.

The Romantics can hence be credited with introducing a further "democratization" in literature, by stretching the limits of convention and choosing protagonists from the fringes of society. But there was one stipulating factor that kept the Romantics well within the bounds of the acceptable literary code of the time. Although the Romantics created heroes who were *outwardly* questionable or even depraved, these same characters always turn out to be *inwardly* pure and full of merit. It was as if to say that it is not important from which segment of society you originate, since nobility of heart can even be found among those in the most squalid surroundings. In some works, there is even the suggestion that it is particularly those who have suffered the depths of shame and debasement who are more likely to know the true meaning of goodness and charity.

Following close on the heels of the Romantics, however, came a new breed of nineteenth-century writer who created a shocking variation on such characters of noble heart. "Realist" writers[27] such as Balzac, Goncharov, and Thackeray were now replacing the character of the meritorious young orphan with a new cynical model. Instead of devoutly earning their entrance into the higher social realms, these young orphans were opportunists who used their wits, cunning, and charm to win the love of unsuspecting aristocrats, and through them climb the ladder to power, money, and social success. Prime examples of such types are Becky Sharp in Thackeray's *Vanity Fair*, Aleksandr Fyodoritch in Goncharov's *A Common Story*, and Charles Grandet in Balzac's *Eugenie Grandet*. Of course, the character type of the opportunist was not new to literature.[28] But what was indeed new was the fact that this type of character was now presented with a high degree of sympathy. This is because these characters were primarily presented as products of their environment—an environment which in truth did *not* permit the poor and disenfranchised to rise out of the squalor no matter how pure of heart they proved to be. Moreover, this new "realism" portrayed most of civilized society as a closed circle offering no opportunities for those outside a small privileged class; the only way to gain entrance to this elite society was through plotting, scheming, and deceiving. The message to be derived from this literature became increasingly clear: in an immoral society, one must become immoral oneself in order to "succeed."

What then was the fate of true love among the Realists? Love stories, alas, became hardly love stories at all, at least in terms of what was previously recognized as such. Many of the stories and novels composed by Realist writers actually do *begin* conventionally, showing a young orphan earnestly trying to win the love of one above his station. But these stories take a new turn: instead of fighting the intractable social obstacles blocking his path, the young orphan, in utter frustration, casts aside his idealism and abandons his idea of winning his love, deciding that the key to all "success" is money and power. And the only way to obtain these things in an unjust society is by being smarter and shrewder than the other man. In such literary works, love now becomes merely the means to an end, with the final implication being: who can believe in love anymore in a world that is unjust and unloving?

In retrospect, one can now say that the relatively mild distrust of civilized society introduced by the Romantics in their attempt to uncover the "natural" man was later intensified by the Realists into a more radical version of the same, but with entirely new consequences. Accompanying the Realists' newfound contempt for society came an equal contempt for its conventions; this combination fostered an attitude toward romantic love that can only be called cynical. Following from this, it seems reasonable to conclude that when faith in man and society are steadfast, love too can flourish. When faith in man and society are lost, love becomes a futile goal, not only untenable but illusory.

From the hard-nosed realism of such nineteenth-century writers, it seemed but a short step to the alienation and existential angst of the twentieth century, phenomena which would ultimately cause the traditional love story to sink even further into obscurity and obsolescence. In the final hour, nonetheless, a valiant attempt was launched by a group known as the "Neoromantics"[29] to recapture the romantic spirit of an earlier period, and with this the classic love story made a sudden unexpected reappearance in the late nineteenth century.

But this was a relatively short-lived resurrection. No one, it seemed, could stem the tide of twentieth-century "progress," whose advocates turned a cold shoulder to romance and dismissed most love stories as mere naive sentiment. And as the traditional love story increasingly became an object of scorn to the sophisticated "literati," it eventually scurried off shamefaced to a corner for good. But the love story refused to disappear completely. Banished from most serious literary endeavors, it now became the stuff of "popular literature," finding its audiences through such venues as the dime novel, cheap theatricals, and later the soap opera.[30]

Lest it seem that this transition in literature was a swift and reckless one, let us make clear that this was certainly not the case. The demise of the traditional love story was indeed bound up with the rise of the twentieth-century movement known as "Modernism." However, Modernism as a general societal phenomenon did not develop suddenly but was the result of a gradual cumulative process. In fact, the growing distrust and eventual rejection of traditional forms usually associated with Modernism should be properly viewed as the consequence of a long chain of events developing simultaneously in the spheres of history, philosophy, politics, and science.

So too was Modernism as a *literary* phenomenon the result of a gradual development, whose influences undoubtedly derived from all the above spheres. It is my view, however, that the chief influences upon Modernism in literature were intellectual ones, and it was the work of three thinkers in particular—Marx, Nietzsche, and Freud—who indirectly brought about the biggest changes in literature, and who ultimately struck the near-fatal blow to the love story as well.

The Deconstruction of Love in Modern Thought

The growing discontent with conventional society already felt by many intellectuals and writers provided fertile ground for the radical political and economic theories presented by Karl Marx. If nothing else, Marx's theories offered a "scientifically" argued rationale for advocating that which previously might have been pondered, but which no one dared to utter—the complete overturning of "bourgeois" society and all it implied. In essence, Marx's theory propounded that revolution was not only a desirable goal, but a necessary dialectical outcome of man's economic enslavement to a corrupt system. Needless to say, this belief had a numbing effect on literature in general, for it threw into question the entire basis of Western civilization upon which its literary products had been built.[31] But in the case of the love story, it seems nothing could more undermine its conventions than such a theory. This is because at the core of the love story there rests the belief that *love* is the cure for society's ills, not social revolution.

Moreover, the focus away from the individual and toward the "masses" stressed by Marx would eventually spell doom for those stories aimed at portraying the singular heroic character overcoming all odds and achieving love and happiness in society. For those possessed by Marxist fervor, the focus on the individual was a dangerous distraction from *the masses* as a whole who in a sense were now becoming the only "hero" allowed to be in desperate straits. Not only was writing about individuals a useless exercise, but it was now intolerable to suggest that individuals could possibly save society (or themselves) through such "bourgeois" notions as love.

Nietzsche continued the attack on the individual, but from a totally opposite standpoint. To him, the individual could not possibly present any serious threat to society's grand destiny as mapped out by Marx, since Nietzsche viewed the individual of his era as dismally weak, ineffectual, and thoroughly lacking in any truly grand visions. Hence his pronouncement that "God is dead" was not so much a declaration as it was a command to the individual to rouse himself from his languor and subservience to foolish and petty goals. But Nietzsche's was not a command that beckoned a return to the traditional God of either Judaism or Christianity; on the contrary, he held these religions largely responsible for creating the "midgets" he saw around him. Instead, Nietzsche found his ideal in an ancient pagan model of man who had once created valiant myths of grand proportions. According to Nietzsche, man can again reclaim such heroic capabilities through the dynamic assertion of his will alone. Through this "will to power" he can take the place of the God who once reigned and be a "creator" himself, forging his own path through the wilderness and reaching heights of valor not known since ancient days.[32]

One would think that if such declamations by Nietzsche had made a powerful impact on the literary sphere, then these surely should have inspired a dramatic resurgence of the traditional romance featuring mighty heroes, rescued maidens, and the like. True, there is evidence that Nietzsche's ideas did influence some artists in this direction (Wagner's operas are the most obvious example),[33] but this was not Nietzsche's lasting legacy. In fact, his theories ultimately proved to have the opposite effect on literature. Instead of bringing about the return of heroism and glory, Nietzsche's ideas opened up a gaping abyss from which there was no easy escape. This is because instead of inspiring confidence in man's new omnipotence, Nietzsche's pronouncements led to an ever-increasing doubt, fear, and resignation about man's *insignificance* in a "Godless" world.[34]

This crisis of faith presented a mighty challenge to the literary artist, who now had to struggle hard to sustain an adherence to conventional forms while the "void" appeared at every turn. Dostoyevsky tackled the problem head-on in *The Brothers Karamazov*, yet he was still able to maintain the semblance of a somewhat conventional novel, perhaps because of his ultimately Christian answer at the end. But in the works of Franz Kafka, the loss of God in the universe seemed to bring with it the loss of everything fixed and regular. This is never more apparent than in *The Trial* and *The Castle*, wherein Kafka is compelled to begin the merciless demolition of literary convention in order to appropriately convey his nightmarish vision of a meaningless universe.[35]

Needless to say, the traditional love story, with all its pristine faith and good will, could hardly survive the assault on the Divine without becoming barely recognizable itself. Indeed, if one should ever think that a world without God brings about a confident humanism, then one should think again. Without assurance that there is Divine order in the universe, romantic love in literature begins to quickly capsize. At its lowest, love is portrayed as a joke or a sham, hardly worth the time for "smart" people (as ironically shown in Thomas Mann's *Buddenbrooks*).[36] At its highest, love is depicted as something that is desperately pursued in order to fill the void with some sort of meaning, imperfect though this may be (as seen in some of the works of Evelyn Waugh, Graham Greene, and Franz Kafka).[37] But even this attempt is so very flawed from the start that despair is the usual outcome.

Notwithstanding all the above, it was actually the work of Sigmund Freud that delivered the final blow to all convention previously governing literature. Nietzsche may have "freed" man from his weak God-"dependence"; but Freud came along and took all that was left—man—and rendered him virtually helpless against the forces that control him. These threatening forces, however, are not external to man, but according to Freud are *internal* forces that dwell in man's own unconscious mind and determine his basic character. Moreover, the realm of the unconscious is most significantly formed during infancy and early childhood, when man's tendencies, which are essentially sexual in nature, are firmly established. In essence, Freudian theory reveals man to be but a slave of his inner self, a self which harbors hidden passions that he must learn to understand rather than repress, lest this lead to severe psychological disorders.[38]

The impact of the Freudian conception of man upon literature was ultimately cataclysmic. With an air of finality, it succeeded in laying to rest the Romantic view that man's inner self is essentially good and pure. In fact, the Freudian conception of man presented an exact reversal of this view, seeing man's basic nature as driven by dark erotic passions deriving from primal incestuous desires. Although this may sound as though Freud was merely returning to

a more sober view of man's passions reminiscent of the Neoclassical period, Freud added a radical new twist which, more than anything else, set him worlds apart from his eighteenth-century an-
tecedents. Using the ancient Oedipal myth as his model, Freud
dislodged the sexual taboo against incest by claiming that all men,
rather than possessing a natural revulsion against incest, are in fact
subconsciously guilty of desiring its fulfillment. Thus, instead of
returning to the classical view that man has a natural abhorrence of
craven acts such as incest, Freud asserted that what man innately
desires is the unhampered expression of such dark passions.[39]

All of this proved to be a mixed blessing for literature. On the
one hand, it gave way to a virtual explosion of creative portrayals
of the human psyche, never before undertaken so expansively on
the written page. (For example, the works of D. H. Lawrence,
James Joyce, Marcel Proust, William Faulkner, etc.).[40] This was all
done with the zeal of the pioneer, armed with the confidence that if
what is *hidden* within man is even more important than what is
apparent, then there remains a vast unexplored territory of dark
motivation and intention to be scrupulously studied, analyzed, and
portrayed. On the other hand, the unconscious mind that these
depictions uncovered pointed to a realm of illogic and obscurity so
arcane that the literary portrayals tended to become inaccessible
and unintelligible to most readers. James Joyce's prose is an obvious case in point, especially in such novels as *Ulysses* and
Finnegans Wake.[41] Here, the creative attempt to capture the
workings of the unconscious mind caused all literary conventions
to collapse, to the point where even grammar and syntax broke
down. In the end, it resulted in a literary product that was barely
comprehensible, at least in terms of previous categories and canons
of literary understanding.

All things considered, the Freudian view of man had a generally
dispiriting effect on man and his literary output alike. Reversing
Nietzsche's overweening confidence in man's potential for creative
freedom through human will alone, Freud's theories emphasized
man's subjection and enslavement to forces beyond his control.
The result, therefore, was a souring of belief in man, and a distinct
reversal of the humanistic optimism that had been steadily building
from the time of the Renaissance to its height in the nineteenth cen-

tury. In the creative sphere, the consequences of this turnabout were so widespread and pervasive that literary works were virtually taken over by gloomy portrayals of self-doubt, fatalism, and resignation about the whole "human enterprise." Indeed, it can be argued that it was Freudian theory that began the questioning of the whole purpose of literature, and which eventually led to the undermining of the written word as intrinsically meaningful, a view later apotheosized by Deconstructionism.[42] This is because Freudian theory introduced the idea that the true story of man dwells within his unconscious, and if that is the case, then how can literature, which had always been seen as an enterprise largely of the conscious mind, even begin to communicate what man is unable to grasp about himself?

The love story understandably suffered the most severely of all the genres, since Freud's theories made eros his prime target, thereby overturning society's prior and closely-held beliefs about the *sanctity* of love. With love now reduced to unconscious sexual motivations, the idea of romantic love became no more than a relic of past ignorance and naivete about the "true" nature of man as revealed by Freud. Nevertheless, the love story did survive within twentieth-century fiction, but in a highly transformed state. Let us make clear, however, that these stories are generally not, as one might expect, a literary celebration of man's newfound awareness of his sexual nature (although such stories do exist). More often, the stories of love are in fact stories of resignation, mourning the *loss* of man's ability to love at all.

The writer who arguably explored this theme most thoroughly of all was D. H. Lawrence. Despite the sensual portrayals of sexual discovery in his work, there is a message of futility that emerges through the "bliss." His novel *Sons and Lovers* is a good case in point, in which the depiction of obsessive attachments and Oedipal complexes leaves the reader with an overriding sense of the hero's permanent inability to love. Even with sexual freedom, there is little hope that the determining unconscious forces can ever be fully overcome or that a successful romantic relationship can ever be truly realized.[43]

In general, the shift from pure romantic love to sexual love became standard in literature as Freud's views of the sexual basis of man's consciousness became a tacit belief of the twentieth-century literati. And along with this new view of eros as darkly and incestuously originating in infancy, the classical structure of romantic love in literature was duly undermined, having previously depended on the traditional notion of eros to sustain it. Without the traditional view of eros that defines love as pure and ennobling (usually traced back to Plato),[44] the familiar stories of the chaste pursuit of the beloved culminating in marriage began to falter and lose all credibility. Instead, with the Freudian influence firmly entrenched, we may still see characters full of longing for romantic union, but they are rarely able to overcome the powerful influence of their unconscious minds that drives them in unseen directions, away from the bonds of true love and commitment.

The Absence of Love in Jewish Literature

Now that we have explored how love has evolved in modern literature from its classic formulation to its recent overturnings, let us return to our primary concern and ask where *Jewish* writers fit into this historical development. Were Jewish writers influenced by the same intellectual trends and societal changes as were their non-Jewish counterparts? Were they beset by similar problems and crises? Did they undergo the same stages of literary development as did other Western writers?

Before attempting to answer these questions, it must first be pointed out that the phenomenon of imaginative literature among the Jews is a relatively recent development, not having truly begun until the middle of the nineteenth century. Therefore, it is impossible to make an exact study comparing the parallel literary development of Jewish writers and non-Jewish writers because Jewish imaginative literature hardly existed while the likes of Cervantes, Shakespeare, Milton, and Swift were defining the genre.

One can, however, argue that Jewish writing did basically undergo the same changes as did general Western literature, only it did so *later* and in a highly accelerated form. In fact, a number of Jewish literary historians have asserted that Jewish writers managed to traverse the road from Classicism to Romanticism to Modernism within a mere seventy years.[45] But before accepting this somewhat facile theory too hastily, I believe it should first be asked how similar in actuality were these proclaimed likenesses of development, and whether it was even possible for Jewish literature to have undergone the same changes when the internal circumstances of the Jewish communities were often so different from those of the surrounding population. Only after answering this will it be possible to ask the following questions: did the love story created by Jewish writers follow the same patterns of development as did the Western love story? Or was the Jewish love story an entity unto itself, with its own history and separate set of internal criteria?

As previously mentioned, the emergence of modern literature among the Jews occurred approximately in the middle of the nineteenth-century, with the first writer of truly original talent being Mendele Mocher Seforim (pseudonym of Shalom Yakov Abramowitz).[46] Writing in both Hebrew and Yiddish, Mendele blended satirical wit with a unique flair for authenticity of characterization, resulting in works that at once express both the pathetic and the grotesque. Should we conclude then that Mendele's creations imitate or parallel the similarly complex satires of Swift, Sterne, and Fielding, even though Mendele lived more than one hundred years later? Although there is no doubt that Mendele and these writers were influenced by similar ideas of "enlightenment" (even though the Haskalah did not reach eastern Europe until the early nineteenth century), it is a vast oversimplification to categorize Mendele's work as merely a Jewish version of European early Enlightenment prose.[47] Let me explain why this approach is problematic.

Some historians of Jewish literature are quick to draw parallels between their own writers and the great writers of Western literature, presumably believing with all good intentions that they are simply elevating Jewish writers to their deserved place among the "gods." There are, however, two problems that grow out of this. First, there is the implication that Jewish writing has no greatness on its own if it is not tried and tested in the larger arena of Western literature. Second, there is the tendency to contort and "disembody" Jewish literature in order to understand it according to Western criteria, rather than allowing it to speak in its own voice and establish its own independent patterns of development. Getting back to Mendele, his prose serves as a good case in point. Viewed on its *own* terms, Mendele's writing can be seen as an outgrowth of many factors that in fact have no parallels within the general society. For example: the suffering of Jewish life in exile, cut off from one's ancestral homeland; the social, economic, and spiritual poverty of "ghettoized" existence; and the psychological weight of bearing an ancient religious tradition and its effect upon the freedom, morality, and imagination of the individual.

In fact, it is my view that as long as Jewish writers continued to write from within the particularity of their own civilization, then Jewish writing can only be properly understood if it is seen as a separate category of literary expression inhabiting a distinct creative territory of its own. To be sure, there were vital links between some Jewish writers and their non-Jewish contemporaries, including the fact that many Jewish writers were known to be both voracious readers and dedicated translators of Western literature into Jewish languages. Nevertheless, this seemed to have its effect more as an influence on the style and structure of their work rather than on the substance.

The separate nature of Jewish literature is all the more apparent when it comes to considering the love story. Where are the Jewish equivalents of Samuel Richardson, Jane Austen, the Bronte sisters, and Walter Scott? Where are the tales of love betrothed and love betrayed, love till death and love beyond the grave? In other words, did Jewish literature, even as it established itself, develop a tradition of the modern love story equivalent to that found in the Western novel? One discovers quite quickly that one has to search very hard to find serious examples of romantic love among the classic writers of modern Jewish prose because the plain truth is that it hardly existed.

Granted, on the most popular level, there did exist Jewish tales of romance. Some of these, such as the *Shmuel Buch*, dated as far back as the fifteenth century and were widely circulated among the Jewish population, maintaining their popularity right into the modern period.[48] But these can hardly be considered developed works of literature in the modern sense, having more in common with the medieval tale than the modern novel. In fact, works such as the

Bove Buch and its later nineteenth-century version, the *Maase Buch*, are basically Yiddish reworkings of a famous medieval English romance, and therefore hardly original as Jewish literature. All the more questionable are the nineteenth-century love stories by the Yiddish writer Shomer, whose immensely popular novels served as the romantic potboilers of the day. Using implausible characters caught in utterly fantastic plots, Shomer's work earned such a negative reputation among serious writers that it can perhaps be said that he singlehandedly did more to discredit the legitimacy of the love story than almost any other factor.[49]

The only real example of a sophisticated piece of literary prose in which the theme of romantic love is truly central is Abraham Mapu's novel *Ahavat Zion* (1853).[50] But here the exception only seems to prove the rule. Despite the overwhelming popularity and groundbreaking position of this work as the first modern novel written in the Hebrew language, it did not succeed in establishing a new genre of the Hebrew love story, perhaps because it did not produce any heirs of comparable or lasting artistic value. True, Hebrew writers such as Smolenskin and Braudes did weave love stories into the plots of their Haskalah novels.[51] But love somehow always seemed contrived to serve the didactic social aims of these works, thus making love seem strained and artificial.

Except for Mapu's singular success, love stories just did not seem to naturally fit in with the present life of the Jews, or with their literary attempts to create an imaginative vision of it. Even *Ahavat Zion*, the main love story written in the early stages of modern Jewish literature, was set in *biblical* times, rather than in nineteenth-century Eastern Europe. Does this then indicate that such stories of love and valor presuppose a settled, autonomous society, and that only out of such contexts do romantic heroes and heroines arise? Does this also imply that the "unnatural" conditions of Jewish life in the Diaspora virtually serve to prevent the very possibility of such epic plots, heroic characters, and grand passions?

Indeed, the *lack* of the love story within the realm of modern Jewish literature was a sore point for Jewish writers of the time, and was a seeming inadequacy of which they were all too self-consciously aware. Mendele laments this very fact in his bitterly ironic monologue on the subject in *Fishke the Lame*:

> Lord of nations! What is this? Is this what it means to be lovesick? I have heard of such things happening, but I have never really been able to understand them. To be smitten by love was to us the same thing as being sick, as having a fever, as being possessed by a dybbuk, or being in a delirium, as having melancholia, or epilepsy. When we talked about love, we used to hold our eyebrows, spit seven times and make a pious face, saying: "It shouldn't happen here! May Jewish children be protected from it!" We also used to laugh at someone in love just as we laughed at the village idiot. . . . Love affairs and marriages for love are customary only among the upper and lower classes. The rest of us folks of a middling sort, have our minds in a bowl of borscht! We're too busy earning our daily bread, trying to make a living. We are not lords or noblemen. We have no time to pay attention to such foolishness. We are Jews, merchants, traders, storekeepers, busy with our business.[52]

Even Sholom Aleichem, who tried in most of his early novels[53] to write serious love stories about Jews, ended up turning away from this genre to find his natural calling as a satiric realist and humorist. In fact, the type of stories at which Sholom Aleichem excelled (and which also brought him his greatest acclaim) were his vivid tales of simple Jews who for the most part had little to do with lofty notions such as romantic love. The main exceptions are of course the stories of Tevye's daughters who, following the modern style, break with tradition and choose their own mates out of love. But even here, the focus of these stories is not on romantic love *per se*, but on Tevye and the development of *his* character, i.e., how Tevye bends to modernity, and how Tevye cleaves to tradition. The inner life of the daughters and their desired mates is only hinted at and never explored in depth, almost as if Sholom Aleichem felt uneasy about depicting passions such as love and therefore kept them at arm's length. Or, perhaps he wisely sensed that the disparity between his small town heroes and the loftiness of the passions was too wide a chasm to bridge, so he merely avoided their head-on meeting altogether. The critic Ruth Wisse is also struck by this curious "bashfulness" in Sholom Aleichem, as she elucidates in the introduction to *The Best of Sholom Aleichem*:

In general, Sholom Aleichem did not do well with a direct approach to the great, climactic, and decisive moments of plot.
When he did attempt a big love scene, or a tough social confrontation, he could be surprisingly inept. You have only to
look at one of his earliest efforts, the thinly disguised autobi-
ographical novella where the wealthy young heroine, who has
been playing fantasies by moonlight, rushes through the garden. and into the arms of her indigent tutor to the following
momentous dialogue:

He: Polinka!

She: Rubovsky!

Impossible to read the scene without laughing—at the author's
expense. It is not that Sholom Aleichem avoided the romantic
subject, the heroic possibility, the grand style of the novel: he
was simply unconvincing and demonstrably *uncomfortable* in
this mode, especially at the high points of resolution, and of
course, conclusion.[54]

But as much as Sholom Aleichem embraced the "smallness" of
the Jews as their supreme virtue, certainly writers who came later
became much less sanguine about this simple native "charm." In
particular, those writers who chose to compose in Hebrew as opposed to Yiddish were increasingly inclined to reject the gentler images of the Jew in favor of bolder and more complex images. Instead of the Jew as small shopkeeper, crusty scholar, or bumbling
dreamer, the Hebrew writers offered new Jewish prototypes such
as the rugged laborer, the freedom fighter, and, for the first time, the
urban, alienated intellectual.[55]

One might think that with these new heroes would also come
new possibilities for Jewish stories about love. Indeed, love does
often blossom in the stories by the young Hebrew writers, but unfortunately it rarely comes to fruition. Most historians of Hebrew
literature explain this phenomenon as being simply due to the fact
that these writers were finding their voices at a tumultuous time in
history (the late nineteenth and early twentieth centuries). Thus,
according to this view, Hebrew writers were influenced by the
same social, political, and philosophical trends as were other
European writers at the time, trends that were eroding belief in

most traditional concepts, including that of romantic love. To a large degree, these historians are probably correct in declaring the influence of Western ideas as responsible for shaping much that is modernistic and experimental in modern Hebrew prose. To be sure, reading Joseph Chaim Brenner is sometimes not that different from reading Dostoyevsky, and strains of Chekhov, Strindberg, and Hamsun can at times be heard in the works of Gnessin and Agnon alike.[56]

Notwithstanding all of this, the example of Agnon remains a constant reminder that despite the general applicability of this approach, it fails in this most decisive case to explain the perplexities of his work. As I have been presenting heretofore, the case of Agnon is arguably the most complex of all the Hebrew writers, since his writing is deeply rooted in a form of Judaism of the most pietistic sort despite his ample utilization of modernist ideas and techniques.[57] This combination of perspectives, so oddly dissimilar in nature, makes it impossible to regard him as yet another twentieth-century modernist who just happened to use the Hebrew language. By the same token, we should not be tempted to go to the opposite extreme of seeing him as a religious zealot whose use of modern literary devices serves pietistic or even mystical purposes.

Consequently, when considering the problem of love in Agnon's work, it is essential to see it not only as part of the larger problem of love in the twentieth century, but also to understand it as part of Agnon's specific view of romantic love (or the lack thereof) within Jewish society as a civilization unto itself. The fact that love almost always fails in Agnon's fictional world cannot be separated from Agnon's overall critique of Jewish society, whose shortcomings seem just as much to blame for the problem as are the passive characters such a society produces. At the same time, this not does not obviate Agnon's profuse devotion to the very people he criticizes so doggedly.

Obviously this is a tension in Agnon's work that seems utterly contradictory on the surface but which makes sense if one attempts to grasp the larger picture. In my view this inherent dualism in Agnon follows closely in the tradition of that dual-imaged persona created by Shalom Abramowitz, Mendele the Book Peddler, who was forever venturing forth into the world while at the same time bearing the weight of holy texts upon his back.[58] Like this image, the pious Jew and the worldly Jew were Agnon's constant though sometimes bitter companions. But that which sustained Agnon, and kept him from sacrificing one for the other, was a vision of a "normal" life for the Jews, where tradition and culture need not clash but can live harmoniously together. In such a vision, Jews will someday take control of their own fate, be heroic as in the days of old, and create love stories that they can believe in as true possibilities for themselves and not just as borrowings from another culture.

In Agnon's lifetime, this vision of course had its practical manifestation in Zionism and the enormous task of bringing about Jewish "normalcy" through statehood. On a spiritual level, Agnon's fiction in a sense shared in this task, since he too seemed to want to transform the Jewish people internally. But it was not without difficulty that he went about this work, since as a true literary artist his critical eye was unsparing in exposing the weaknesses of his fictional subjects. Hence, Agnon's love stories are not idealized pictures about what love should be, but rather are sadly ironic portraits of what it is not. In this sense, we discover that Agnon's paradigmatic statement on love, his novel *Sipur pashut*, gives us a bird's-eye view of all he finds lacking in Jewish society, and of what he sees as ultimately holding it back from its complete "liberation." If nothing else, reading this synoptic novel by Agnon tells us that love cannot flower in a society that is disjointed and discontent. But perhaps understanding what Agnon sees as the cause of the illness is the first step toward understanding his cure.

Notes

1. Love figures prominently in most of Agnon's long novels, especially in *Temol shilshom* and *Shira,* as well as in the novella *Shevu'at emunim.* Though not central to the plot, love serves as an important symbolic element in the novel *Ore'ah nata lalun,* as represented by the marriage of Rachel and Yeruham (and later Erela and Kuba), even though the emotions of the individuals involved are barely explored.

2. See *Sipur pashut* in *Kol sipurav shel Shmuel Yosef 'Agnon,* 1st edition, vol. 5 (Berlin: Schocken, 1935); and 2nd edition, vol. 3 *'Al kapot haman'ul* (Tel Aviv: Schocken, 1953). Note that in the second edition of Agnon's collected works, arranged by the author himself, many of Agnon's most important love stories appear in volume 3 alongside *Sipur pashut,* such as "Bi-dmi yameha," "Ha-rofe u-gerushato," and "Panim aherot."

3. For example, see Gershon Shaked, *Shmuel Yosef Agnon: A Revolutionary Traditionalist,* trans. Jeffrey Green (New York: New York University Press, 1989), 130; and Dan Miron, "Domesticating a Foreign Genre: Agnon's Transactions with the Novel," trans. Naomi B. Sokoloff, *Prooftexts* 7 (1987):1-27. Miron makes the point that *Sipur pashut* is "the novel with almost perfectly wrought structure" (8).

4. By "traditional," I mean those works depicting a pristine love relationship usually leading to marriage, as exemplified in such works as Samuel Richardson's *Pamela* and Jane Austen's *Pride and Prejudice.* Paralleling this genre, but sometimes viewed as an entirely separate type of love story, are those novels more in the "courtly" tradition such as Flaubert's *Madame Bovary* and Tolstoy's *Anna Karenina.* These works generally stress passionate longing for one who is unattainable, sometimes culminating in adultery, and have their origins in such medieval tales as the story of Tristan and Iseult, or Lancelot and Guinevere. For an excellent discussion of "courtly love," see Irving Singer, *The Nature of Love,* vol. 2 (Chicago: University of Chicago Press, 1987), 19-126.

5. See Northrop Frye, *Anatomy of Criticism* (Princeton: Princeton University Press, 1957). It is important to make it clear from the beginning that I base much of my discussion on Frye's "archetypal" or "mythic" approach to literature, following his insight that literature is in essence a retelling and reworking of several basic narratives. The love story is one such narrative, possessing its own specific structure, which Frye traces back to the Greeks and calls "domestic comedy" (*Anatomy,* 44-45, 163-71). Although I have not been using Frye's term (opting instead for the simpler term "classic love story"), I follow Frye on the specific aspects of the classic love story structure which I outline in detail on pages 4-5 above. For a similar use of the term "classic love story," as well as a discussion of this genre as it particularly applies to the novels of Jane Austen, cf. David Lodge, *After Bakhtin: Essays on Fiction and Criticism* (London: Routledge, 1990), 116-28. See also Peter Gay, *The Bourgeois Experience* (Oxford: Oxford University Press, 1986), vol. 2 ("The Tender Passion"), 135-39, for a sociologically based view of the love story, which Gay calls the "governing preoccupation" of the modern novel, particularly that of the nine-

teenth-century novel. Cf. also Ian Watt, *The Rise of the Novel* (Berkeley: University of California Press, 1957), 135-38, 148-49, 154, 164-67, 172-73. Watt quotes Dr. Johnson as defining the novel as being in essence a "small tale, generally of love" (64). In a similar vein, Joseph Epstein's tribute to the late Isaac Bashevis Singer quotes Singer as saying, "All stories are love stories." Cf. "Our Debt to I. B. Singer," in *Commentary* 92, no. 5 (November 1991), 34.

6. For a highly informative discussion of Modernism and how it is manifest in literature, see Irving Howe, "The Idea of the Modern," in *Irving Howe: Selected Writings 1950-1990* (New York: Harcourt Brace Jovanovich, 1990), 140-66. Cf. also the essay by Harry Levin, "What Was Modernism?" in *Refractions: Essays in Comparative Literature* (New York: Oxford University Press, 1966), 271-95.

7. This reflects a recent trend among historians of Hebrew literature. For example, Yair Mazor's work entitled *The Triple Cord: Agnon, Hamsun, and Strindberg* (Tel Aviv: Tel Aviv University Press, 1987). Also cf. Hillel Barzel, *Beyn Agnon le-Kafka, Mekhkar mashveh* (Ramat-Gan, Israel: Bar-Ilan University Press, 1972).

8. By this I mean to say that choosing to write in Hebrew inevitably tied the early Hebrew writer to certain premodern assumptions, which have to do with Jewish sociology, psychology, history, and religion, no matter how secular and rebellious that writer tried to be. I attempt to illustrate this point more fully below, for (as will be made clear) it is one of the central themes of this work.

9. Although I see Agnon as the best example of this point, I believe that this generally holds true for other Hebrew writers of his day such as Brenner and Gnessin.

10. I consider *Sipur pashut* to be Agnon's classic statement on love and its multifarious complications for the Jew in the modern world, whereas his love stories merely explore one or two of the issues at stake. Therefore I believe that a proper understanding of this novel provides a key to the understanding of the other stories about love. Although it could be argued that a novel such as *Temol shilshom* (*Only Yesterday*) is an equally important statement on love, I would argue that although love plays an important role in the novel, it is not the central issue, but is rather symbolic of the restless search of the hero for his identity.

11. Frye, *Anatomy of Criticism*, 43-45, 163-71.

12. See Robert Alter, *The Art of Biblical Narrative* (New York: Basic Books, 1981), 47-62, especially 54-56.

13. See Robert Scholes and Robert Kellogg, *The Nature of Narrative* (London: Oxford University Press, 1966), 226.

14. For a detailed discussion of the Cinderella tale and its many versions and variants, see *Cinderella: A Folklore Casebook*, ed. Alan Dundes (New York: Garland, 1982). Cf. also Iona and Peter Opie, *The Classic Fairy Tales* (London: Oxford University Press, 1974), 117-27.

15. Note should also be made of the midrashic reference in Rashi (1040-1105) to an apparently well-known love story, whose original rabbinic source has been lost. This is known as the tale of "the weasel and the well" (*hulda vabor*), a story that in the Jewish popular imagination might well have had com-

parable power to that of the Cinderella tale. This ancient Jewish love story tells of a young couple who meet by seeming chance, and who make a vow of love that is witnessed by no one but a weasel and a well. This vow is later broken, and the girl and boy are then separately visited by a series of misfortunes which do not end until their original vow is honored, and they are finally wed. See *Treatise Ta'anit of the Babylonian Talmud*, ed. and trans. Henry Malter (Philadelphia: Jewish Publication Society, 1978), 104-7, and especially note 130.

16. Although Fanny Price is not technically an orphan (her parents are alive), she is sent away due to poverty to live with her rich and aristocratic relatives who become her de facto "parents" for most of her childhood and adolescence. Since all of the other aspects of the story are so similar to the "Cinderella structure," it surely qualifies as a classic of the genre.

17. A good example of this can be seen in the Yiddish play "The Dybbuk," by S. Anski, in which the pledge made between two men to have their children betrothed leads to tragic consequences when the vow is broken. See S. Anski, "Der Dybuk," in *Gezamelte Schriften*, vol. 2 (Warsaw: An-Ski, 1925), 7-105. For the newest English edition of this classic Yiddish play see *The Dybbuk and Other Writings*, ed. David Roskies, and trans. Golda Werman (New York: Schocken, 1992).

18. For a fuller discussion of this tendency, see Frye, *Anatomy of Criticism*, 165-170.

19. Singer, *The Nature of Love*, 101.

20. By "democratic spirit," of course I do not mean this in an overtly or exclusively political sense, but in the social sense that loosens the definition of *worthiness* to include one from any level of society who merits recognition and ultimately happiness. See Lodge, *After Bakhtin*, 117, who uses the term in a similar sense when discussing Richardson's *Pamela*.

21. The Neoclassical period is usually defined as beginning in 1660 and ending in 1789. For a general discussion of Neoclassicism in literature, see chapter 1 of Walter Jackson Bate, *From Classic to Romantic* (Cambridge, Mass.: Harvard University Press, 1949), 1-26.

22. Romanticism is generally seen to have begun in 1780 and to have ended in 1850. See Jacques Barzun, *Romanticism and the Modern Ego* (Boston: Little, Brown, 1943), 197.

23. For a thorough overview of European Romanticism, see Rene Wellek, "The Concept of Romanticism in Literary History," in *Concepts of Criticism* (New Haven: Yale University Press, 1963), 128-98. For some good brief discussions of the Romantic era, see: Frederick Artz, "Neoclassicism and Romanticism," in *From the Renaissance to Romanticism* (Chicago: University of Chicago Press, 1962), 219-82, especially 222-27; and J. B. Priestly, "Rousseau and the Romantic Age," in *Literature and Western Man* (New York: Harper and Row, 1960), 113-21.

24. Artz, *From the Renaissance to Romanticism*, 240-66.

25. See Walter Jackson Bate, "The Growth of Individualism: The Premise of Feeling," in *From Classic to Romantic* (Cambridge, Mass.: Harvard University Press, 1949), 129-59.

26. Irving Babbitt traces this trend back to Rousseau. See Irving Babbitt, *Rousseau and Romànticism* (Austin: University of Texas Press, 1977), 118-19. For examples of prostitutes taking a sympathetic role, see Marie in Flaubert's *Novembre* (1842), Sonia in Dostoyevsky's *Crime and Punishment* (1866), Marguerite Gautier in Dumas's *La Dame aux Camelias* (1852), and Esther Gobseck in Balzac's *Splendeurs et Miseres des Courtesanes* (1847), who is, interestingly, both a harlot and a Jewess!

27. Realism in literature is generally seen to have occurred between 1850 and 1885. For a learned discussion of the distinction between Romanticism and Realism in literature, see Northrop Frye, "The Context of Romance," in *The Secular Scripture* (Cambridge, Mass.: Harvard University Press, 1976), 35-61. For a thorough overview of Realism in literature, see Wellek, *Concepts of Criticism*, 222-55. Cf. also Barzun, *Romanticism and the Modern Ego*, 138-51.

28. Certainly one need only think of a figure such as Mr. Wickham in Jane Austen's *Pride and Prejudice.*

29. The period of Neoromanticism in literature is generally regarded as occurring between 1875 and 1905. See Barzun, *Romanticism and the Modern Ego*, 154-59. Some examples of Neoromantic writers are Hugo von Hofmannsthall (1874-1929), Edmond Rostand (1868-1918), Anna de Noailles (1876-1933), and the early Knut Hamsun (1859-1933).

30. It should be mentioned, however, that some serious writers in the twentieth century still wrote fairly conventional love novels, such as Virginia Woolf in her early novel *Night and Day* (1919), and E. M. Forster in his *A Room With a View* (1908). But novels such as these did not hold a mainstream position, and as time went on they became further marginalized within the higher spheres of artistic taste. For a thorough discussion of the melodramatic genre, see Frank Rahill, *The World of Melodrama* (University Park: Pennsylvania State University Press, 1967). See especially the Introduction, entitled "Setting the Stage," pp. iii-xviii. Another view of this subject can be found in the controversial but classic work on love by Denis de Rougemont, *Love in the Western World* (Princeton: Princeton University Press, 1983), 232-35.

31. As Jacques Barzun aptly put it: "Marxist Leninism lies behind much of this energy to achieve a liberating blankness . . . [and] leads logically to destroying the contents of any institution connected with the past." Jacques Barzun, *Classic, Romantic, and Modern* (New York: Anchor Books, 1961), 143. See also the essay by Stephen Spender in *The God That Failed* (London: Hamish Hamilton, 1950), 231-72, and especially 269-71.

32. For a succinct discussion of Nietzsche's philosophy, especially "the death of God," see Erich Heller, "The Importance of Nietzsche," in *The Artist's Journey Into the Interior, and Other Essays* (New York: Random House, 1965), 171-98.

33. Although there is some controversy over whether it was Nietzsche who influenced Wagner or vice versa, it is well known that they had once been devoted friends until they had a falling out that led to mutual hostility. Notwithstanding these biographical facts, it is clear that they had many ideas in common, especially the passion for a revival of the ancient myths in their grandest

form. See Jacques Barzun, *Darwin, Marx, Wagner* (New York: Doubleday Anchor Books, 1958), 231-317.

34. Irving Singer sums it up well by saying, "Nietzsche's philosophy embodies the malaise of his time and our own. He effectively shows us what is no longer tenable in beliefs about men, women, and their erotic being." Irving Singer, *The Nature of Love*, vol. 3 (Chicago: University of Chicago Press, 1987), 70. In a related way, M. H. Abrams seems to detect a direct line of descent leading from Nietzsche to Jacques Derrida and Deconstructionism, for as he puts it, "In this aspect of his dealings with language, Derrida's writings present variations on a Nietzschean theme: Absolutes, though necessary, are dead, therefore free play is permitted." See M. H. Abrams, "How to Do Things with Texts," in *Partisan Review* 46 (1979): 570. Cf. also Frederick Copleston, "In Criticism of Nietzsche," in *Friedrich Nietzsche: Philosopher of Culture* (London: Burns, Oates, and Washbourne, 1942), 195-205.

35. For a brief but insightful discussion of this tendency in modernist literature (especially how it applies to Kafka and T.S. Eliot), see Gabriel Josipovici, "Modern Literature and the Experience of Time," in *The Modern English Novel*, ed. Gabriel Josipovici (London: Open Books, 1976), 252-72. Cf. also the penetrating essay by Anthony Thorlby entitled "Kafka's Narrative, A Matter of Form," in *Kafka and the Contemporary Critical Performance*, ed. Alan Udoff (Bloomington: Indiana University Press, 1987), 30-40.

36. In *Buddenbrooks* the heroine Tony blithely rejects the man she loves, and instead dutifully marries men whom she is convinced it is smart to marry because of their presumed wealth and social status. Although her marriages fail, Tony apparently learns nothing from her mistakes and continues to blindly value material security above all else by attempting to arrange a marriage of convenience for her daughter.

37. For example, Evelyn Waugh, *Brideshead Revisited*; Graham Greene, *The Heart of the Matter*; Franz Kafka, *The Castle*. In line with the direction of my argument, Erich Heller states the following, in reference to Kafka's hero of *The Castle*: "In K's relationship to Frieda the European story of romantic love has found its epilogue. . . . Intermixed with his erotic craving, inarticulate, diffuse, and yet dominating it, is the desire for spiritual salvation. Even a 'happy ending' spells profound disillusionment for the romantic expectation. Perhaps it is Strindberg, deeply admired by Kafka, who wrote the last chapter of its history. It is certainly Kafka who wrote its postscript." Erich Heller, "The Castle," in *Franz Kafka*, ed. Harold Bloom (New York: Chelsea House Publishers, 1986), 133-49. Also, Irving Howe describes this type of phenomenon (in reference to Dostoyevsky) as follows: "The love-seeker or God-seeker is particularly vulnerable to self-torment if he inwardly believes that he seldom experiences true love and that instead of embracing God he merely celebrates his own ego. This is a central ambivalence of neurotic character—one is almost tempted to say of modern character." Irving Howe, *Politics and the Novel* (Cleveland: Meridian Books, 1957), 54.

38. See Sigmund Freud, *A General Introduction to Psychoanalysis* (New York: Washington Square Press, 1924), 304-8; 319-47.

39. For a succinct study of the effect of Freud on literature, see Frederick Hoffman, "Freudian Theory," in *Freudianism and the Literary Mind* (Baton Rouge: Louisiana State University Press, 1975), 1-42. Cf. Lionel Trilling, "Freud and Literature," in *The Liberal Imagination* (New York: Doubleday Anchor Books, 1954), 44-64. Cf. also Harold Bloom, "The Internalization of Quest-Romance," in *Romanticism and Consciousness* (New York: Norton and Co., 1970), 3-24. In this essay, Bloom discusses what he calls Freud's "erotic pessimism" and says, "in the Freudian view, all erotic partners are somewhat inadequate replacements for the initial sex objects, parents" (14).

40. In particular, see D. H. Lawrence, *Sons and Lovers* and *Lady Chatterley's Lover*; James Joyce, *Ulysses* and *Finnegans Wake*; Marcel Proust, *Remembrance of Things Past*; and William Faulkner, *As I Lay Dying* and *The Sound and The Fury*. Of course, these are merely a sample of the numerous works that could fall into this category.

41. Roger Moss in fact argues that the only way to truly penetrate Joyce's work is to accept that the obscure nature of the work is intentional and the difficulties cannot be disposed of in order to understand it. In other words, he argues that the language cannot be deciphered but must merely be "confronted." See Roger Moss, "Difficult Language: The Justification of Joyce's Syntax in *Ulysses*," in Josipovici, *The Modern English Novel*, 130-48.

42. For a broad and incisive overview of how modern trends in literary theory have had a generally deleterious effect on the interpreting of literature, see Gerald Graff, *Literature Against Itself* (Chicago: University of Chicago Press, 1979). Cf. also: Robert Alter, "Introduction: The Disappearance of Reading," in *The Pleasures of Reading in an Ideological Age* (New York: Simon and Schuster, 1989), 9-22; M. H. Abrams, "How to Do Things with Texts," in *Partisan Review* XLVI (79): 566-88; and Alvin Kernan, *The Death of Literature* (New Haven: Yale University Press, 1990), for a particularly critical assessment of the effects of Deconstructionism on literature.

43. Despite Lawrence's well-known criticisms of Freud, there are striking similarities in their basic representations of sexuality and the unconscious. For a convincing presentation of this very point, see Philip Rieff, "The Therapeutic as Mythmaker," in *D. H. Lawrence*, ed. Harold Bloom (New York: Chelsea House, 1986), 31-58.

44. See, for example, Plato's *Symposium* 204-206, for a description of love as a desire for the good. For a thorough discussion of Plato's concept of love and its implications for literature, see Irving Singer, "Platonic Eros," in *The Nature of Love*, vol. 1 (Chicago: University of Chicago Press, 1984), 47-87.

45. I concur with Gershon Shaked who views the influence of Western culture on modern Hebrew literature as complex and dialectical in nature. He states, "There is no direct exchange of content from any European current to its Hebrew parallel. It is not even always affected by geographical propinquity. . . . These [Western] influences do not depend on time or place; they are not definitive literary schools. If on occasion a specific literary trend becomes noticeable in a certain writer's works, the impact is diffused and absorbed into the literature, which evolves according to its own rules." Gershon Shaked, "Jewish Tradition

and Western Impact in Hebrew Literature," in *The Shadows Within* (Philadelphia: Jewish Publication Society, 1987), 88.

46. The writers who preceded Mendele tended to write in the zealous spirit of the Enlightenment, thereby producing works that were highly didactic and generally somewhat lacking in artistic merit.

47. It is probably more likely that if anyone influenced Mendele, it was his Russian contemporary, M. Saltykov-Shchedrin, who was known for his biting satires of Russian society.

48. First published in Augsberg in 1544, the *Shmuel Buch* is thought to have been composed in about 1450. Its author is unknown.

49. See S. Niger, *Dertzeyler un Romanisten* (New York: "Cyco" Bicher-Farlag, 1946), 84-95. Cf. also Sholom Aleichem's satire entitled *Shomer's Mishpet* (Berdichev, Russia: Spector, 1888).

50. Some historians of Hebrew literature (e.g., Lachower) consider the eighteenth-century plays by Rabbi Moses Hayyim Luzzatto (1707-46) to be the first works of modern Hebrew literature. Indeed, in the plays *Migdal Oz* and *La-Yesharim Tehillah,* the love story serves as an integral feature of the plot structure. However, it is my opinion that it is difficult to categorize these works as pieces of *modern* literature, since they were apparently written as mystical allegories rather than as artistic expressions. See Fischel Lachower, *Toledot ha-sifrut ha-ivrit ha-hadashah,* vol. 1 (Tel-Aviv: Dvir, 1946-8), 14-44.

51. See for example Braudes's novels *Ha-Dat ve-ha-Hayyim* (1885) and *Shetei ha-Kezavot* (1888); and Smolenskin's novels *Simhat Hanef* (1872) and *Ha-To'eh be Darkhei ha-Hayyim.* (1876).

52. *Fishke the Lame,* trans. Gerald Stillman (New York: Thomas Yoseloff, 1960), 175-77.

53. See, for example, Sholom Aleichem's novels *Stempenu* and *Yosele Solovey.*

54. Ruth R. Wisse (with Irving Howe), "Introduction," *The Best of Sholom Aleichem,* eds. Irving Howe and Ruth R. Wisse (New York: Simon and Schuster, 1979), xxv.

55. See Simon Halkin, "New Directions in Palestinian Literature," in *Modern Hebrew Literature* (New York: Schocken, 1970), 111-30.

56. See Robert Alter, *The Invention of Hebrew Prose* (Seattle: University of Washington Press, 1988).

57. In his article on Agnon's ambivalent relationship to the modern European novel, Dan Miron makes the case for viewing Agnon as a literary genre unto himself—what he terms "a unique Agnonesque gestalt." See Dan Miron, "Domesticating a Foreign Genre: Agnon's Transactions with the Novel," *Prooftexts* 7 (1987): 1-27.

58. For a thorough discussion of Mendele's persona, see Dan Miron's work, *A Traveller Disguised* (New York: Schocken, 1973).

Chapter 2

Agnon the Social Critic:
The "Successful" Society and the Stifling
of Personal Freedom

If indeed Agnon's premier work on love is the novel *Sipur pashut*, then one would hardly expect to encounter a work that seems to argue so forcefully *against* the power of love. After all, his hero Hirshl goes "mad" for the sake of it, his heroine Blume is left alone because of it, and in the end Hirshl's and Mina's firstborn son is "abandoned" as a result of it. And this is all because of a youthful attraction between a boy and a girl that in the end had nothing to do with what Agnon ostensibly presents as a far more important task—adjusting to the conformities of Jewish middle-class life in turn-of-the-century Galicia.

But if Agnon's work contains any message, it is "let us not be fooled by appearances alone." In fact, I would contend that despite appearances to the contrary, love is not rejected by Agnon, nor is it cast off with a wistful sigh about the naive idealism of youth. If anything is glaringly amiss in the novel, it is not love, but the *society* within which Agnon sets his love story.[1]

On this note, it could be said that from a sociological perspective, Agnon's main antagonist in the novel is neither Hirshl's overbearing mother Tsirl, nor even the lame-headed Mina whom he is pressured to marry. Rather, it is the town itself, Szybusz (and perhaps all others like it), that is the prime "culprit" acting as the source for all that goes wrong in the story and perpetuating the ensuing cycle of unhappiness.[2] Indeed, Szybusz is so essentially flawed that even a simple love story cannot be told about its inhabitants. It is as if the novel is telling us that even when an author tries to write a love story about members of such a society (as Agnon strives mightily to do), it cannot be told seriously, and it slips into irony and farce from the very outset.

Hence, the irony of the title is not so much about whether this story is simple or not (as most critics take it to mean). More precisely, the novel's irony lies in the fact that when a Jewish writer tries to tell the most simple of stories natural to any society—the love story—he fails miserably, even though this should be the easiest of tasks. But Agnon is not merely poking fun at the ludicrous futility of this venture, for there is something of a bitter undertone to the novel, suggesting something further: if only the Jews could become a nation like all other nations, then maybe they could also tell simple stories without having to always descend into self-mockery and buffoonery.

Consequently, the role that the *social* plays in this novel to undermine the success of the love between Hirshl and Blume is of crucial importance for understanding Agnon, especially in case we are tempted to think that the problem of love in Agnon's work is limited to psychology alone. It is clear from *Sipur pashut* that Agnon took the facts of Jewish social reality very seriously, and he portrays some of its more dismal manifestations in painstaking detail. What saves the novel from heavy-handedness and outright gloom is, of course, Agnon's use of irony, which not only breaks the tension, but at times almost conveys a tone of casual lightheartedness, thereby allowing Agnon's otherwise scathing critique of Jewish society to sink in insidiously and perhaps even more powerfully than if he had expressed it overtly. But, as is always the case with irony, what remains difficult is the task of disentangling the irony from the seriousness.[3] This can only be achieved by holding up the subtle details of the text for close and careful scrutiny. We will then be able to determine how the problem of love in *Sipur pashut* is directly connected to the distinct characteristics of the society that Agnon depicts. In fact, it will be a study of these characteristics that will give us a clearer idea of what exactly it is about this society (and perhaps diaspora Jewish society in general) that impedes the progress of love and prevents it from ever coming to fruition.

One of the first aspects of the social reality of Szybusz that the reader encounters is that there exists among the Jewish inhabitants a strict social hierarchy with its own set of rules and expectations. At the top of the social ladder stand families such as Hirshl's, the Hurvitz family, who belong to a merchant class of Jews that consider themselves among the top families, for no other apparent reason than that they possess money. It is interesting to note, however, that there is hardly a reference in the novel to another type of Jew who had traditionally occupied *the* honored place in Jewish society—the rabbi or scholar. Agnon barely explains this transformation in the scale of Jewish values from reverence for scholarship and piety to that of exclusive respect for economic success, letting the reader reckon for himself how this could have come about. He only offers us such few lines as: "Indeed the study of Torah had lost its old prestige, so that many young Jewish boys nowadays were putting their religious books aside and turning to more useful occupations." (14 [3:65])[4]

Entering this social setting is the penniless and recently orphaned Blume Nacht who, having just lost her mother, is now totally dependent on her only living relatives, the Hurvitz family. Although she is taken into their home, she is speedily ushered into the role of maidservant by Tsirl (much in the same way that Cinderella is made into a lowly servant by her wicked stepmother after her father dies). This new status as "maid" effectively shuts out Blume from fitting in with *any* of the social groups of the town. On the one hand, not only is Blume an educated young woman, but she is a blood relative of the respected Hurvitz family, so she does not fit in with the lower social class of townsfolk which includes maids and servants of various kinds. On the other hand, even though Blume is a relative of the Hurvitzs, she is now relegated to serving as the household maid, so that she is not given any of the privileges enjoyed by family members.

Indeed, in Blume's case, being a "family member" is more of a liability than an advantage, for she is even more exploited than the usual servant by an unjust master. The worst of it is that she is not

paid any wages whatsoever for her work. But to Tsirl, the auto-
cratic head of the Hurvitz household, this is completely justified,
as is reflected in her piously hypocritical remark: "[Blume] is one
of us, isn't she? He who rewards us will reward her too." (7 [3:59])
Even the suggestion by the narrator that Tsirl will surely provide
Blume with a dowry one day and thereby recompense her for her
labor (8 [3:59]) is patently ironic, for not only is Tsirl excessively
miserly, but she has also seen to it that Blume's chances of marriage are slim. This is because Tsirl has placed Blume in a contradictory and thus untenable social role as both relative and maid,
therefore ensuring that she fits nowhere in the social hierarchy of
the town. Whom could she possibly marry that would befit her
station? As she is a member of the esteemed Hurvitz family, a
suitor who is merely a servant would be beneath her. By the same
token, a gentleman coming from a respectable middle-class family
in a town with such socially rigid conventions as those prevailing in
Szybusz would certainly never consider marrying a mere
housemaid.

There is ostensibly a third Jewish social class in Szybusz of
which Agnon often makes mention in the novel, comprised of the
politically active young Jews who affiliate either with the Zionists
or the Socialists. But lest we think that this signals a new direction
for Jewish society, Agnon lets us know from the beginning that
both of these groups, at least in their "Szybusz form," hold out little hope for a transformation of Jewish life.[5] In fact, Agnon deri-
sively portrays the youth who attend the clubhouses of these
movements as lacking in any real seriousness about their respective
causes. These young people of generally well-to-do backgrounds,
and "supported by their parents" (14 [3:65]), are mockingly described by Agnon as joining these movements mainly as a leisure
activity, i.e., to eat, socialize, play chess, and read the newspapers
(17 [3:67]).

It is no wonder, then, that Blume Nacht is offered no alternate
social venue or chance for escape from her hopeless social circumstances through these particular groups. Moreover, this may at
least partially explain why the attentions of the young Zionist en-
thusiast Getzel Stein are ignored by Blume. This should not surprise the reader in the least, given the fact that Agnon has made it

sufficiently clear in the novel that the Zionists of Szybusz, including Getzel, are generally a laughable bunch. Not only are they not seriously committed to social change for the Jews, but they are shown to be idlers and dilettantes who may mouth Zionist sentiments and slogans, and weep at Zionist hymns (17 [3:67]), but who are ultimately unwilling to make any personal sacrifices for the sake of their "beliefs." By the same token, Agnon makes it very unlikely that a man of truly heroic character could possibly emerge from this vapid social crowd in order to rescue the distraught young Blume from her wretched and lonely plight.[6] Unlike the Cinderella story, *Sipur pashut* presents us with no princes who are filled with the stalwart spirit needed to be able to defy social convention and fight for their beliefs, whether it be for national independence or for the woman they love. Blume has no prince on her horizon, and Agnon leaves the reader with little hope that, at least in this society, she could ever find one.

We mentioned earlier in our discussion that in *Sipur pashut* Agnon barely refers to that figure in Jewish society who had at one time been enshrined at the top of the social hierarchy, i.e., the rabbi or scholar. But there is one notable exception in the novel whom Agnon does describe in a fair amount of detail, and this is the character of Hayyim Nacht, Bluma's late father. From Agnon's description, however, the reader would be unlikely to view Hayyim Nacht as particularly meritorious or worthy of high honor, for he is presented by the narrator as he is seen through the eyes of the people of Szybusz—as a wastrel and a complete failure. That is, there is barely a hint that at one time such a man likely would have been revered for his serious dedication to study and scholarship, not to mention his meticulous honesty. Instead, he is castigated in the novel for committing one of the gravest sins among the sons of Szybusz—having no "business sense":

> Hayyim Nacht was not well-off like Boruch Meir Hurvitz, nor was he regarded especially highly by others; for though he was a well-read and cultured man with a gift for languages, his education, like that of all the Nacht family, far outstripped his attainments. And though Mirl had married him with her father's consent, the old man never stopped reminding her vindictively that, having failed to win the heart of a successful businessman, she had to settle for a spendthrift of a scholar

who frittered away her whole dowry without earning a penny
for himself. (19 [3:69])

Indeed, Hayyim Nacht was unable to support his family financially, but we discover only a few paragraphs later that this is not because he was a "spendthrift," but to the contrary, it was because of his unflinching honesty. Here, in fact, is a good example of where the reader can easily disentangle Agnon's irony from his serious commentary. Agnon lets the true facts of Hayyim Nacht's life speak for themselves, despite the narrative trick of (ironically) taking on the petty and scornful "voice of Szybusz." And these are some of the startling facts about Hayyim Nacht's life that begin to emerge: first, when Hayyim Nacht tried his hand at business, his partners took advantage of his trusting nature and stole all his capital. When he subsequently tried to secure a teaching job, he was unsuccessful due to his refusal to use bribes and flattery (20 [3:70]). Even when he was reduced to becoming a private tutor for children, the parents of his few pupils eventually withdrew them because he did not teach anything practical "like bookkeeping" (20 [3:70]). As a result, Hayyim Nacht ended up spending the later years of his life in a state of melancholy, fully aware of the tragedy of his existence in this society that had no place for men like him. The worst of it was that in order to remain true to his own beliefs and scruples—"A man does what he has to do" (22 [3:71])—he was forced to sacrifice his family's material well-being in the process. Perhaps as a logical consequence of all of this suffering inflicted on him by a society that made a man of learning, talent, and decency into the object of scorn and ridicule, Hayyim Nacht finally died prematurely of "sorrow and humiliation." (22 [3:71]).

As we mentioned previously, however, it is likely that a pure scholar such as Hayyim Nacht would have been revered in an earlier Jewish society, before the days when the acquisition of money became the highest ideal.[7] Put in mythic terms, it is as if Hayyim Nacht resembles a king who has lost his throne to a corrupt regime, and he and his family are forced into poverty and degradation despite the nobility of their blood. It is perhaps no accident, then, that Blume's "superior" qualities in the novel do not emerge out of nowhere, but go back to the fact that she is Hayyim Nacht's daughter, and like her father she must live among the lower classes of society despite her "aristocratic" origins. Indeed, she is like the princess in the fairy story whose father has been robbed of his kingdom, and who must await the arrival of her noble knight to rescue her and reestablish her rightful place in society, and thereby turn society into a just place again.[8] But in this Jewish version of such a tale, not only is the knight she chooses of feeble nature, but the society itself is inherently weak. This societal weakness, however, does not so much stem from corruption as from a kind of lethargy that perpetuates a life of dullness and mediocrity, so that any attempt at a radical awakening would likely go unnoticed.

It is dullness and mediocrity in fact that pervade the entire social atmosphere of Szybusz, to the extent that even the modern changes that have come to the town are more lamentable than laudable. It could even be said that at times modernization has brought with it a kind of moral decay. Rather than replacing the apparently outmoded tradition of the past with anything vital or dynamic, some of the modern "innovations" that Agnon describes seem only to shrink the social fabric of the town, leading its inhabitants toward petty preoccupations and even vulgar displays of their growing decadence. For example, the young men of Szybusz have now taken to boasting of their sexual exploits without any sense of shame, modesty, or discretion (27 [3:76]), while some are reputed to keep entire "harems" of loose young women who sell sexual favors for a high price (135 [3:180-81]). Even the town's leading citizen, Sebastian Montag, keeps his own coterie of women (85 [3:133]) whom he refers to superciliously as his "nebbichlach,"[9] notwithstanding the fact that he has a wife and often serves as the cantor at the town's Great Synagogue (212 [3:254]). To make matters worse, some of the intellectuals of the town have begun to fraternize with the lewd wandering minstrels who regularly visit Szybusz. Although Agnon lets the reader know that these wanderers are nothing but crude entertainers who "sang songs put to bawdy lyrics" (28 [3:76]), these minstrels are looked upon as fascinating objects of sociological study by the naively enthusiastic intellectuals of Szybusz. As the narrator puts it: "Students strolled with them in public, and referred to them as artists, drank with them in the taverns, lectured on them and their folk songs." (28 [3:76])

Although the Jews of Szybusz increasingly give free rein to their "lower" instincts in the name of modernity, they nonetheless reserve a special place for those things they consider to be worthy of their "higher" selves: that is, anything or anyone that is somehow connected to Germany and its *kultur*. For example, the reader learns that the young people of Szybusz are in the habit of reciting German poetry to one another as part of their courtship, although the narrator makes a point of hinting that the seriousness of their devotion to Schiller and Lessing is somewhat less than their appreciation for the lengthiness of the poems. In other words, what better excuse could the youth of Szybusz find to justify spending long stretches of time together in mixed company than engaging in such a "respectable" activity as reciting the tropes of classical German verse! (75 [3:123]) Similarly, Agnon pokes fun at the fact that Mina begins to call Hirshl by the German name "Heinrich," under the influence of the more worldly-wise Sophia Gildenhorn (97 [3:144]). This endeavor by Mina to endow Hirshl with an air of German sophistication cannot help but strike the reader as humorous, not only because it is attempted by such simplistic a means as changing a name, but especially because Hirshl clearly lacks any resemblance to a man of cool precision and cultivated taste that would characterize the prototypic German man of culture. A similar irony can be seen in the attitude of the townsfolk toward the wedding of Hirshl and Mina. To the people of Szybusz, the outstanding feature of this illustrious wedding is not the ceremony, the music, or the trimmings, but the fact that they had the honor of having in attendance an actual relative from Germany, who, as it happened, stumbled upon the wedding by accident when he was passing through town. Not only that, but this cousin of the Ziemlich family is hardly a paradigm of German sophistication and culture. Although Arnold Ziemlich's presence elicits high excitement among the townsfolk, he is nothing more than a shrewd egg dealer who regards Szybusz as an untapped source of fresh eggs for export to eager German households.

In a parallel light, Agnon's portrayal of the townsfolk's naive awe and admiration for anything modern or enlightened is brought into sharp relief in his depiction of the honor bestowed upon the town's idiosyncratic matchmaker Yona Toyber. The degree of self-deception practiced by the folk of Szybusz is only magnified by the fact that although Toyber has gained his lofty reputation by virtue of ostensibly being a modern scholar, he is in actuality nothing more than an ordinary matchmaker who once wrote a single article that was published in a modern Hebrew journal on the subject of geography (a subject hardly likely to inspire a fevered response!). Agnon in fact lets the reader know in no uncertain terms that Toyber's article was actually a rather outlandish piece of writing, apparently meant to be about geography, but filled at the same time with Toyber's own brand of "homespun philosophy" (37 [3:86])—that is, bearing little or no resemblance to a true work of modern scientific reasoning and rational persuasion. The inhabitants of Szybusz, however, do not seem to notice this. They also do not seem to notice that Toyber has not published anything else ever again, nor has he spent his time in the pursuit of knowledge or modern enlightenment. On the contrary, as the town matchmaker he serves one of the most traditional functions in the community. This is an ironic contrast that Agnon surely creates in order to emphasize that the people of Szybusz may like to fancy themselves as modern, but in truth are still firmly attached to traditional modes of social behavior that govern their more practical concerns, such as who may marry whom on the social ladder. If the matchmaker is an enlightened "scientific" scholar, how much easier it is to utilize his services without being seen as hopelessly traditional and narrow-minded.

In a society where self-deception seems to be the rule of thumb, it is no wonder that an ordinary matchmaker like Yona Toyber should be elevated to a place of high repute, while a true scholar such as Hayyim Nacht and his daughter Blume have been denigrated and scorned. It is as if the entire society is topsy-turvy, with the fools holding seats of honor while the scholars are treated with contempt.[10] How could a match be made for Blume that is not equally topsy-turvy? How could love break through the barriers of social class when the classes themselves are based on faulty and oftentimes foolish ideas of status and worth? Moreover, how could love hope to succeed when the idea of love itself is so completely misunderstood in a town like Szybusz? In order to make this very point, Agnon gives the reader a few choice examples of how the people of Szybusz mistakenly (and comically) define "true love":

> There were people in Szybusz who swore that the apogee of true love was a certain rich lady in town who had run off with her butler and refused to return to her imploring husband even though her new lover beat her. There were others who told you to look for it in the person of the unrepentant Mottshi Shaynbart, who had lost his leg chasing after a woman and now had a wooden one in its place. Still others insisted that only the man driven out of his senses by passion could claim to be love's acolyte. In each of these cases, the passion for love misled them about love itself. (43 [3:91-92])

In a manner strikingly similar to the attitude toward love satirized by Mendele Mocher Seforim, (quoted in chapter 1 above),[11] it is clear that the people of Szybusz regard love as something only for the rich, the foolish, or the mad. In this way, we see that despite their enthusiasm for anything "modern," the townsfolk have never truly given up the traditional concept of the arranged marriage, and most of the practical considerations that go along with it, i.e., dowry, family status, etc. What they *have* given up, however, is the religious foundation upon which the institution of the arranged marriage is most securely and happily grounded. In fact, this society is left clinging to institutions that have little meaning anymore, even though it pretends to have moved beyond them in embracing the modern world. But Agnon unequivocally shows that the people of such towns have little notion of what being modern really is. The tragedy of it is that they are left neither here nor there—without religion to sustain their adherence to traditional values and institutions, and without sufficient understanding of the modern world that would allow them to truly take their place within it.

Consequently, it is little wonder that Hirshl has nothing to say to refute his mother's argument that love is not the important factor in choosing a mate (46 [3:95]). True, the psychological portrait of Hirshl is one of a weak-willed and callow youth, lacking in the fundamental courage that would be necessary in order to oppose his mother's will in any overt manner.[12] (We will argue in the next chapter, however, that Hirshl's "madness" is a form of rebellion, twisted and covert though this rebellion may be, that he finally stages in order to oppose his mother.) At the same time, it should be understood that Hirshl is not only faced with a formidable mother, but with an entire society that basically shares her beliefs. Tsirl merely has the "knack" for expressing such things bluntly: "A bachelor can be free to follow his heart, but what would the world come to if he didn't put his romances aside when the time came to get married? A fine place it would be if everyone followed their hearts!" (46 [3:95]).

Yet, Agnon does more than merely show how onerous it would be to rebel against the entire social structure of the town in pursuing the woman of one's choice. He also subtly goes on to disclose to the reader that this social structure may exist for at least one good reason: to preserve the frail political status of the Jew in an endemically hostile environment. In this way, Agnon moves beyond being a mere satirist of Szybusz, revealing himself as a writer who understands the *reasons* for the town's moral and social decay even though he may find the decay itself to be repugnant. Agnon in fact repeatedly gives us glimpses of the precarious political status of the Jews in Szybusz vis-a-vis the non-Jewish authorities, and the Jews' consequent need to regularly appease these authorities through bribery (39, 52, etc.; [3:88, 3:101, etc.]). Under these "abnormal" conditions, it is not surprising that the Jews do not have time for such things as love, which would seem to be a luxury designed only for those societies with the security and the leisure to pursue it. With the lowly habits of mere survival so ingrained, the Jewish community clings to its tried and true social structures even though these may have lost all meaning amidst the whirling changes of an increasingly modern world.

Agnon also subtly provides the reader with another reason for the suspicion of romantic love expressed by the inhabitants of Szybusz. They not only fear that it could lead to impractical marriages, but that romantic love could even lead to marriages with gentiles. Although this may have always loomed as a threat to Jewish communities, this would be particularly dangerous now that towns even as unsophisticated as Szybusz have begun to pursue the pleasures of the modern world. Agnon expresses this fact indirectly in his inclusion of one very significant detail in the life of

Mina Ziemlich—that the Jewish headmistress of her boarding school has gone and married a Polish gentile (53 [3:102]). Although the characters in the story respond with shock and disbelief to this occurrence, Agnon had already prepared the reader for such an eventuality in his description of the type of "worldly" young lady that this headmistress produces in her school:

> Even though she [Mina] had grown up in a village she had the graces of a city girl, having gone to a boarding school in Stanislaw where she learned to speak French, embroider, and play the piano, so that nothing about her so much as hinted that she was the daughter of country Jews. When she accompanied her parents to Szybusz, her elegance contrasting with their simplicity and her leisurely gait with their hurried one, one might have thought her the daughter of a Polish nobleman besieged by two Jewish peddlers. The transformation undergone by her was so complete that her own father and mother scarcely seemed to belong to her anymore. Not that she was ashamed of them—it just could not be said that she was particularly proud of them either. (41 [3:89])

Despite the inclusion of such legitimate reservations about the modern world and its threat to Jewish continuity, Agnon on the whole presents a highly critical view of Szybusz in *Sipur pashut*. Not only is it a town mired in its own petty preoccupations, but its Jewish inhabitants lack both the courage and the will to fight for any changes to improve their lot. Indeed, the self-appointed "social leaders" of the town spend most of their time idly seeking material pleasures. But these "social leaders" are not the usual high-ranking citizens that one might expect to find at the top of the social register, but are a diverse group of pleasure-seekers led by none other than a travelling insurance salesman and his wife, by the fitting name of Gildenhorn (i.e., "golden horn" or "horn of plenty"). Comical as this may seem, the Gildenhorns are a force to be reckoned with, having successfully made their home the center of Jewish social activity in the town by offering an abundance of free food, drinks, and card games. The group revolving around the Gildenhorns have in fact gained social ascendancy in the town by an extremely powerful ploy: they invent comic nicknames for the rest of the townsfolk. In this way, they have not only succeeded in setting themselves up as arbiters of taste, but they have done so by instilling fear in the hearts of the local population, who live in dread of becoming the next victim of one of their comic monikers. Although the full extent of the Gildenhorns' detrimental influence is only hinted at in the novel, Agnon makes it clear that they are more than partially responsible for the corruption of the social atmosphere of the town. As the narrator states outright:

> Indeed the decline and fall of Szybusz's old patricians had begun on the day that Gildenhorn moved into town. Anything went in Szybusz these days, and every rogue felt free to raise his head; nor could anyone do anything about it, since half the local residents were afraid of Gildenhorn and the other half were on his side. (55 [3:103])

With the social climate of the town thus determined by the playful malice of such a crowd, it becomes understandable why noble pursuits and heroic ventures do not abound in Szybusz. Surely any serious undertaking would quickly become the butt of jokes and the object of ridicule by these self-appointed critics. So too would romantic love also be an unlikely event in such an atmosphere, for not only is love a matter of serious intent, but it requires at least one confident pursuer in order to come to fruition. In this tainted climate where character is constantly maligned, self-confidence would certainly be eroded and self-dignity put in constant doubt. It is no wonder then that Hirshl is as nervous as he is upon entering the home of the Gildenhorns on what is to be the fateful eve of his accidental "engagement" to Mina (59-60 [3:108-9]).

In fact, Agnon's brief description of the Gildenhorn crowd, coupled with Hirshl's reaction to it, gives the reader a sense of the insidious nature of Jewish self-hatred and the "schlemiel" syndrome that seems to result from it. In other words, the type of joking and mockery that may begin as a playful pastime can end up creating a debilitating climate for those who come under its cloud. It is a bitter irony, however, that this social atmosphere is created by the Jews themselves who, instead of trying to change their society for the better, indulge in a kind of mockery of their fellow Jews, and end up promulgating an unhealthy form of self-negation that is

at least partially responsible for producing weak-willed offspring
such as Hirshl.

In this light, the story of Hirshl could be read as a simple tale of
a naive youth who is burdened with an acute case of self-doubt and
social awkwardness produced largely by the menacing social atmosphere that surrounds him. Note the type of neurotic delusions
that begin to grow within Hirshl the longer he stays at the Gildenhorns' party:

> The more he smoked the stupider he felt, and the stupider he
> felt the more he smoked. The befuddling odor and taste of the
> tobacco mingled with the heavy smell of grease coming from
> the kitchen made him gasp for air. He was afraid that he
> would disgrace himself by throwing up or fainting. The cards
> jumped so quickly from hand to hand that, strangely enough,
> the hands themselves had disappeared. Then the cards van-
> ished too and there was nothing but little red and black faces
> dancing mockingly in front of him. (57 [3:105])

It is at this party in fact that the reader begins to give up all
hope that Hirshl will live up to the role of romantic hero carved out
for him so teasingly by Agnon in structuring the story according to
the "Cinderella mode." (Wealthy son of a leading family falls in
love with his beautiful cousin who is an impoverished orphan,
much to the chagrin of his wicked mother who tries to thwart the
union.) Instead, the reader witnesses the transformation of Hirshl
into a "schlemiel" who allows himself to be accidentally betrothed
to Mina, an event which happens *to* him rather than at his own be-
hest.[13] Because of this pivotal event, and Hirshl's spineless acceptance of it, what should have been a simple love story about Hirshl
and Blume ends up becoming a study of a neurotic young man who
despises himself and his life the way it is, but who has neither the
motivation to change himself nor the courage to rebel against his
situation. In fact, Agnon seems to be showing the reader that self-
determination and strength of will are as important for the attain-
ment of one's own personal happiness as they are a prerequisite of
political freedom. But in the frivolous and petty hedonistic social
atmosphere of a town like Szybusz, passivity and lethargy (the
accepted modes of behavior) threaten both the political life of the
Jews and the psychological health of the individual. Hirshl, who

had the opportunity to pursue the woman of his choice, tosses away his independence at the Gildenhorns' party, and thereafter becomes a pathetically comic figure clinging to the image of himself in his own mind as a romantic hero, but unable to take any courageous steps to fulfill this role.

One would think that the stagnant social atmosphere of Szybusz would produce a population of Jews who, if not desperate to escape its narrow confines, would surely manifest symptoms of despondency and despair. But except for the singular example of Hirshl Hurvitz, this is not the case at all. In fact, the reader is presented with a portrait of a town which on the surface is extremely content with its lot. And what does Agnon show us to be the main source of their enjoyment of life? Food. Delicious, home-cooked Jewish food. The emphasis on food in all its savory variations and permutations is of course a central irony in the novel, and one which Agnon uses to display the banality of the lives of the people.[14] The reader learns, for example, that the Jewish inhabitants of the town are so emotionally attached to their food that even when some of the more adventurous souls leave Szybusz to live in America, it is the food of Szybusz that draws them back to their hometown, never to leave again (70 [3:119]).[15]

Similarly, when the Hurvitz family is invited to the Ziemlichs' home for dinner to celebrate the engagement of their children, the main object of concern for both sets of parents is not the suitability of their children, nor the religious piety of the prospective families, nor even the practical concerns of an impending marriage; it is the lavish spread of food on the dinner table that is the focal point of the evening (77-81 [3:125-131]). Indeed, the food is the means by which the Ziemlichs try to impress their guests, as well as the yardstick by which the Hurvitzs judge their future in-laws. But Agnon gives the reader a nudge about the emotional temper of the evening by stressing a significant aspect of the table setting—a china gravy dish shaped like a goose with "its beak angrily open"—as if to tell the reader that all is not so right with the celebration despite its outward appearance.[16] At the same time, Hirshl hardly eats anything at this dinner, which can be regarded as part of his weak-willed attempt to rebel against his engagement to Mina.[17] But Hirshl is not able to sustain even this minor rebellion, for at the end of the dinner he succumbs to the luscious dessert: "the aroma proved irresistible. Even Hirshl took a large slice and *ate it with gusto*" (81 [3:129], emphasis added). In a social setting where food is of such supreme importance, eating takes on a significance far beyond its usual worth: eating becomes an act of submission, whereas refraining could have been a first tiny step toward independence.

Even when the serving of food is cast in a romantic light, as in the idyllic scene in the countryside depicting the two families having a picnic in strawberry season, Agnon casts a shadow on the outwardly beautiful scene by showing us how little Hirshl and Mina have to say to one another (92-93 [3:140]). It is made clear that such picnics fail to satisfy the restless Hirshl, who knows that something is missing but cannot say what it is. Note the contrast between the description of the scene and Hirshl's subsequent reflections upon it:

> under Bertha's doting eye, Hirshl sat beneath a tree with his parents, his fiancee, and her father, before him a loaf of yeasty-smelling, appetizing black bread, bowls of butter and cheese, a pitcher of buttermilk, and lots of red berries swimming in sweet cream. Servants smelling of tar and wood waited to do his every bidding, bringing him new dishes, taking away old ones, and filling his empty glass. (92 [3:139-40])

And then:

> Although the world seemed his for the asking, Hirshl felt that he too was sad and that a man might have all the good food, pleasant surroundings, wealth, possessions, honor, and fame that could be wished for, everything but one thing, and still feel that happiness eluded him. What was that thing? If his own father and mother did not know, it was unlikely that anyone did. (93 [3:140-141])

Although Hirshl does not know (or is afraid to admit) what that "one thing" is that he is missing in his life, there is little doubt that it is love. The fact that Hirshl relies on his parents to supply the answer to this question is doubly ironic, because to them happiness is indeed based on those very things Hirshl finds lacking—good food, pleasant surroundings, wealth, possessions, etc. It is in fact Hirshl's weak reliance on his parents and their worldview that leads him to the misguided conclusion that if they do not know the answer then no one else possibly could. Hirshl is unable to see beyond the material goals of his parents' world, with its emphasis on physical comforts (especially those of the stomach), partly because there are few alternatives offered in the society. Blume represents one such alternative, but to have gone the route of love for the sake of a penniless girl would likely have meant having to endure parental and societal disapproval and a probable sacrifice of material comfort. This would surely require someone of sterner stuff than the likes of Hirshl Hurvitz, who has been made "soft" by a society that worries more about acquiring good things to eat than it does about cultivating tough inner qualities, such as courage, strength, and independence.[18] The obsession with food and other material comforts in the novel is in fact another way of demonstrating to the reader how thoroughly the society is mired in trivial matters of the body and how oppressive these things can be in the absence of anything higher. Surely love would have little chance to thrive in such a society, for it is one of those higher pursuits that is virtually incomprehensible to a populace in thrall to the pleasures of the stomach and the comforts of the body.[19]

There is perhaps no better way to determine how the folk of Szybusz rate the importance of love in choosing a mate than looking at whom the town matchmaker himself picks to be his bride. Of all the eligible women in Szybusz (including Blume Nacht), Yona Toyber chooses to marry the spinster sister of Getzel Stein, despite the fact that she is ugly, hunchbacked, and has the temperament of a shrew. The reader in fact is told several times in the novel of her spiteful character and gross demeanor (144,.204, etc. [3:189, 247, etc.]). True, Toyber is burdened with practical needs which might forestall the idea of looking for love, i.e., he is a recent widower with children to care for. This, however, does not explain the fact that he chooses to marry such an exceedingly repugnant woman. Notwithstanding her lack of "higher" virtues (such as compassion, charm, intelligence), even those "lower" considerations such as physical attractiveness seem to have no importance to Toyber, so that one is tempted to conclude that men like Toyber are virtually passionless in matters of sex. Nonetheless, Toyber's choice of a bride should not entirely surprise us, since he picks her precisely because of the one redeeming feature she does possess: she is a devilishly hard worker. For a man like Toyber, this fact alone would be sufficient reason to overlook all her negative traits, because it is made clear in the novel that Yona Toyber is so congenitally lazy that a woman who could do all his work would be all he needs in a woman![20]

Yet the story of Yona Toyber's marriage has an unexpected twist to it. His hunchbacked bride is utterly transformed by her new role as wife and mother. Even her own mother can hardly believe the change in her "monstrous shrew of a daughter" (204 [3:247]) who now happily runs Yona's household with love and dedication. Indeed, she reveals herself as a deeply emotional being who, in her newfound joy, begins to tearfully sing ballads of love and death while she works, as if she herself fears the loss of all she has gained (205-6 [3:248]).

The reader is thus left with the question of what the story of Yona Toyber's marriage indicates about the status of romantic love in Szybusz. This story seems to vindicate the idea of the practical marriage, which unpredictably has the effect of redeeming the wretched life of a bitter hunchback. Does Agnon then intend the reader to apply this standard to the Jews of Szybusz as a whole? Is the marriage of Toyber to the nameless[21] and hunchbacked sister of Getzel Stein the author's ideal of a successful and happy union? To be sure, this seemingly redemptive story of the accursed woman transformed by her new life is the only example we have in the novel of the unambiguous triumph of the arranged marriage. To drive the argument further, if the entire novel is to be seen through the lens of this woman's experience, then this would seem to imply that characters like Hirshl Hurvitz should be regarded as no different than this hunchback, who merely needed to learn that the key to happiness lies in the practical realm of home, marriage, and family.[22]

Although it might appear on the surface that this is the novel's ultimate message, I would argue that Agnon, by including such a story, is in fact making quite the opposite point. Perhaps it is true that individuals as deprived as this hunchbacked woman could find fulfillment in the small rewards that a marriage of convenience might bring—although, truth to tell, as the wife of the self-indulgent Yona Toyber, she is not much more than an elevated household drudge. But this does not mean that for the author of *Sipur pashut* all Jews should be content with such a meager lot. In other words, what is satisfying for a hunchback should not be satisfying for all Jews. In point of fact, this meagerness of vision is precisely what Agnon has been satirizing throughout the novel. If the weight of the irony in his novel carries a single didactic purpose, it would be to open the eyes of his readers and help them see the mire into which Jews sink when they accept the false notion that they are inherently weak and "hunched."[23] Only by seeing this can they hope to do away with the stunting notion that Jews should be content with their lot, i.e., that they should be happily resigned to small goals and petty aspirations.

Moreover, contrary to their own self-negating concept of themselves, the Jews are not in an irreversible state of deprivation and weakness.[24] When at the decisive moment in the novel, the Jewish "hero" Hirshl Hurvitz is given the chance to pursue the woman he loves rather than accept a practical match, he is in essence offered the opportunity to escape from a debilitating life of mediocrity. Not physically crippled, Hirshl need not be bent over like the hunchback but could stand straight if he had the courage and strength of will to do so. But like all the other characters in the novel,[25] he bows his head to the societal pressures and follows meekly after the fold. Romantic love, which could have been the catalyst for Hirshl's liberation, is precipitously dispelled and pushed to the edges of consciousness, only to erupt later in the form of "madness." The reader in fact learns that the only place that love *can* survive is not within this society at all, but on its edges, in the home of Akavia and Tirza Mazal, the couple whose union is the sole marriage of love that is mentioned in the novel (138 [3:160]). It is surely also significant that it is to this home on the edge of town that Blume Nacht escapes. It seems to serve as a welcome haven for a kindred soul who, like the Mazals, cannot find her place in a town such as Szybusz. Perhaps it is also where Blume can at least live vicariously through the happy union of its householders who, unlike anyone else in that society, have freely and courageously chosen to entwine their fate.[26]

Notes

1. There are many theoretical works dealing with the relationship of litera-ture to society. See, for example, Charles I. Glicksberg, *Literature and Society* (The Hague: Martinus Nijhoff, 1972); Harry Levin, "Toward a Sociology of the Novel," in *Refractions* (New York: Oxford University Press, 1966). For works dealing specifically with Agnon's depiction of Jewish society, see Yehuda Friedlander, "ha-Klal ve-ha-prat be-sipure 'Agnon," in *Yuval Shai likvod Shai 'Agnon*, ed. Baruch Kurzweil (Ramat Gan, Israel: Bar-Ilan University, 1958), 61-77; and Gershon Shaked, "Hayyim ba-Nes—Sh.Y. 'Agnon: Dramot ha-hevratiot ve-mimushan ha-sifruti," *Iton* 77, no. 9 (July-August 1985): 22-4.

2. See the article on Agnon and the origins of "Szybusz" by Joseph Bar-El, "Tshatshkis, Agnon, and the Etymology of Shibesh," in *Oksforder Yidish: A Yearbook of Yiddish Studies* 2 (1991), 3-16.

3. For a thorough study of irony in Agnon, see the two major works by Es-ther Fuchs, *Omanut hahitamemut: 'al ha'ironiah shel Shai 'Agnon* (Tel Aviv: Tel Aviv University Press, 1985), and *Sehok samui: Heibetim komiyim ba-yit-sirah ha-'agnonit* (Tel Aviv, Israel: Tel Aviv University Press, 1987).

4. All the pages cited in this work will be from the English translation by Hillel Halkin followed in square brackets by the corresponding pages from the original Hebrew text. See: *A Simple Story*, trans. Hillel Halkin (New York: Schocken, 1985); *Kol sipurav shel Shmuel Yosef 'Agnon*, second edition, vol. 3, *'Al kapot haman'ul* (Tel Aviv: Schocken, 1953). For the convenience of the English reader, I employ Hillel Halkin's spelling of the names of the characters in the novel, with one minor misgiving: I would have preferred to spell Blume as "Bluma," since it would have more accurately conveyed the proper pronuncia-tion to English readers, and would have avoided creating the misleading impres-sion that her name is pronounced "Bloom." Other than this small detail, I be-lieve Halkin's translation to be an excellent rendering of the Hebrew into En-glish. Although I have not referred to it by page number, I would also direct the reader to the superb Yiddish translation of the novel by Eliezer Rubinstein, enti-tled *A Poshete Ma'ase* (New York: Der Kval, 1958).

5. Agnon's story "Bi-n'arenu u-vi-zkenenu" is a satirical portrait of such political groups in Szybusz. It is perhaps significant that this story follows directly after *Sipur pashut* in the volume *'Al kapot haman'ul* in Agnon's collected works.

6. Note for example how Getzel Stein is contrasted (to his disfavor) with the biblical Samson, an ironic comparison that comically highlights the inap-propriateness of juxtaposing the two figures: "Like any red-blooded youth his age, Getzel had not waited for a matchmaker to court the woman of his dreams. He was too shy though, to confess that he needed one, not having the courage of Samson in the Bible, who, charmed by a Philistine wench, told his parents, 'Now get ye her for me to wife'" (219 [3:261]).

7. Another example of this type of disregard for learning can be found in the brief description of the one man in Szybusz who still writes Hebrew poetry.

Note the ironically scornful tone of the narrator: "God in heaven knew what made a young fellow like him care for Hebrew. Did he think it was a ticket to riches and fame?" (211 [3:253]).

8. See my discussion of the Cinderella story in chapter 1 above, especially pp. 4-6. Also see the article by Gershon Shaked, "Bat ha-melekh ve-se'udat ha-em," in *Shai 'Agnon: mivhar ma'amarim 'al yetzirato,* ed. Hillel Barzel (Tel Aviv, Israel: 'Am 'Oved, 1982), 259-92.

9. "Nebḥichlach" is Yiddish for "pitiful ones."

10. Note the similarity here to Jonathan Swift's *Gulliver's Travels,* part 1, "A Voyage to Lilliput."

11. See chapter 1 above, p. 24.

12. Cf. the article by Dina Stern, "Ba'ayot ha-talut ve-hizdahut be-haye Hirshl Hurvitz: 'iyyun sifruti-psychologi be-*Sipur pashut* leShai 'Agnon," *Bi-Sadeh Hemed* 13 (1971): 296-303.

13. There is a distinct echo here of the accidental engagement of Pierre to Helene in Tolstoy's *War and Peace,* book 3, end of chapter 1.

14. It is important to note that the reader's first impression of Hirshl and Tsirl is based on their reaction to Blume's cakes that she brought with her to their home. Hirshl responds with profuse but shy admiration for Blume; Tsirl responds with the decision to exploit Blume's talents (6-7 [3:58-9]).

15. Here, an ironical echo of the biblical story of the Israelites' longing to return to Egypt's fleshpots seems unmistakable.

16. 78 [3:126]. This same china goose reappears later in the novel on p. 227 [3:269] with a similar effect.

17. Hirshl's refusal to eat at the engagement dinner is also a deeper psychological ploy—an attempt (though weak) at rebelling against his mother and her world which is dominated by an over-concern with food. As Hirshl says explicitly at the top of p. 81 [3:129]: "Being hungry has made me realize that it's time I made something of myself. Only how can I make anything of myself when I'm still so dependent on my parents?" This and Hirshl's other attempts at rebellion will be discussed in greater depth in my next chapter. For an insightful discussion of the motif of food in the novel, see the article by Gershon Shaked, "Bat ha-melekh ve-se'udat ha-em," in *Shai 'Agnon: mivhar ma'amarim 'al yetzirato,* ed. Hillel Barzel (Tel Aviv, Israel: 'Am 'Oved, 1982), 259-92.

18. For a similar theme, see the famous Yiddish story by I. L. Peretz, "Bontcha Shveig" ("Bontcha the Silent") wherein the character Bontcha chooses as his reward for a life of suffering a mere roll with butter. In Peretz's day, this story was read aloud repeatedly at workers' meetings as a call for independence from oppression; moreover, it served as a call for liberation from the ingrained meekness and timidity that was seen to characterize the *galut* Jew.

19. As the narrator openly puts it: "if anything held true of the middle-class Szybuszian, it was his greater concern for the needs of the body than for the needs of the soul. And the same went for the working class." (208 [3:251])

20. Toyber's laziness.is emphasized several times in the novel. At one point the narrator even says of Toyber: "Barring war or cholera, anyone with habits like his was sure to live to a ripe old age" (204 [3:247]).

21. It is certainly significant that Toyber's wife, the sister of Getzel Stein, has no name in the novel, as if to suggest that she is so lowly a creature that she does not even merit a name of her own.

22. Certainly many critics interpret the end of *Sipur pashut* this way, i.e., that Hirshl merely needed to learn to accommodate himself to the practical realities of life. For example, see Arnold Band, *Nostalgia and Nightmare* (Berkeley: University of California Press, 1968), 239-54, esp. 251-54; and Hillel Barzel, "Sh.Y. 'Agnon—gilui ve-ne'elam," in *Hikre 'Agnon*, ed. Hillel Weiss and Hillel Barzel (Ramat Gan, Israel: Bar-Ilan University Press, 1994), 131-75, and esp. 154-62.

23. The metaphor itself of "Jew as hunchback" is an old and oft-used one that is resonant with historical significance; it is sometimes employed to represent the bent and oppressed state of the Jew in the *galut*, but more often used as a satiric barb by Haskalah writers. Note that the twentieth-century Yiddish poet Jacob Glatstein revives this metaphor, while turning it on its head, by declaring in his well-known poem "A gute nacht velt" ("Good-Night World") that he *desires* a return to the old "hunchbacked Jewish life."

24. One cannot help but see it as significant that this novel was published in 1935, i.e., only a few years before the Jews of Europe are to be engulfed in flames. Although I am not suggesting that Agnon could have predicted what was about to occur, his novel certainly satirizes the deeply ingrained habits of lethargy that he seemed to see as characteristic of the small Jewish communities of eastern Europe.

25. Although Yona Toyber's case may be viewed as an extreme one, his choice is indicative of the Szybusz mentality that considers most everything in terms of its practical benefits. Another revealing example is that of the teacher Gimpel Kurtz, who marries a housemaid, seemingly because of her talent for cooking and baking. But the reader is given an ironic nudge by the narrator, who tells the reader of the wonders that good cooking can perform. Not only is his wife's cooking the basis for Kurtz's choice of a mate, but it also turns his fate around: she cooks such a tasty dinner for some school officials that she not only saves her husband from being fired as an inept teacher, but they make Kurtz into the headmaster of the school (216 [3:258]).

26. Note the age difference between the Mazals, and the fact that Akavia had been previously in love with Tirza's mother. This is a love match that in traditional society would likely have been frowned upon. See Agnon's story "Bi-dmi yameha," that appears, significantly, just before *Sipur pashut* in the volume *'Al kapot haman'ul*. In his book on Agnon, Shmuel Werses notes the conversely analogous relationship in *Sipur pashut* between Akavia and Tirza Mazal versus Hirshl and Bluma. See Shmuel Werses, *Shai 'Agnon ki-feshuto: kri'ah bi-khetavav* (Jerusalem: Mosad Bialik, 2000), 45-6. Similarly, Stephen Katz, in his study of Agnon's novels, discusses this and other similarly analogous relationships that run through Agnon's works. See Stephen Katz, *The Centrifugal Novel: S. Y. Agnon's Poetics of Composition* (Madison, N.J.: Farleigh Dickenson University Press, 1999), 130-1.

Chapter 3

Agnon the Psychologist (Part 1):
The Prevented Hero and
His Inner Obstacles

The argument that has been developed thus far, that *Sipur pashut* is in essence an imitation of a simple romantic tale that has somehow gone awry (that is, a love story *in potentia* that has been aborted),[1] leads one to see that there are a specific set of reasons embedded within the novel to account for this failure. As we have already observed, the vapid social atmosphere of Szybusz hangs like a pall upon the novel and serves to stifle any potential seed of love from blossoming. However, although the social environment may be the most pervasive cause of love's failure, it is the psychological weakness of the hero Hirshl that is undoubtedly the most decisive cause of love's complete demise.[2] Indeed, Hirshl's frailty as a hero is such that one cannot help but ask how the beautiful orphan Blume Nacht could ever have been attracted to one as patently unheroic as Hirshl Hurvitz. One might be tempted to ask whether Agnon intentionally created a comic figure with all the opposite attributes of heroism in order to parody the idea of a romantic hero and laugh at the very possibility of love and its fulfillment. [3]

In other words, is the creation of Hirshl Hurvitz a mere joke on the reader? There is some evidence to support such a claim, for certainly there is a pathetically comic aspect to this would-be hero, with his endless vacillations between self-doubt and self-importance.[4] Even the name Hirshl Hurvitz has an unmanly ring to it, in its diminutive use of the Yiddish name Hirsh and in the sing-song alliterative confluence of his first and last names.

At the same time, it would be an error to conclude that Hirshl is a clownish figure created merely to mock and undermine the idea of romantic love. In my view, Agnon fashioned Hirshl with too many subtleties and contradictions to allow for such a simplistic interpretation. In fact, I would argue that despite appearances to the contrary, a careful analysis of Hirshl's character gives one ample reason to understand the attraction that Blume feels for Hirshl, even if Hirshl himself is not able to live up to the image that Blume has of him. In this sense, Hirshl possesses what I would call the "potential for heroism," and it is the hope that this potential will be fulfilled which serves to stimulate the reader's expectations and gives the novel much of its dramatic tension.

It is in fact possible to trace what Blume is attracted to in Hirshl from their very first encounter near the beginning of the novel. Although the first view of Hirshl that is given the reader seems mostly to disclose the overly close and almost childish relationship that Hirshl has with his mother,[5] this is immediately undermined by a small but significant act initiated by Hirshl which takes his mother (and the reader) by surprise (6 [3:58]). Hirshl informs his mother that he wishes to tell her a secret and Tsirl dutifully responds to her son's wish by inclining her ear toward him—instead of reproving her son's seemingly childish desire to tell secrets in the presence of their new guest Blume. But it soon becomes apparent that this is a clever little caprice on Hirshl's part, calculated to contradict his mother, and is not at all the game of secret-telling that it seems to be. Instead of actually whispering something in his mother's ear, Hirshl moves close to her ear but then tricks her by speaking in a loud voice and in fact utters something in an attempt to make his mother's previous remark look false. Tsirl had just finished saying that in her household people are not interested in cakes and sweets, obviously attempting to hide from Blume her own greed for such things and perhaps to cover up her budding scheme that Blume become their cook and provide such delicacies. But Hirshl does not let Tsirl's remark go unchallenged, and in a loud voice, so that Blume can clearly hear him, he praises the tastiness of the cakes and tries to get his mother to speak the truth about how good they are. He shouts,"You must admit, Mother, that these cakes are delicious." Tsirl in turn is forced to respond, if only grudgingly, by frowning and uttering, "All right."

Although this scene is short and Hirshl's actions are not large ones, it reveals something about Hirshl that is important for understanding the psychology of his character: though raised by a mother who is cold, ambitious, and slyly domineering, Hirshl nevertheless has a lively seed of rebellion within him. This scene reveals an incipient attempt to break free from his mother's authority in the household, even if his meager act of rebellion fails to effect any lasting changes.[6]

At the same time, the smallness of his action also gives the reader a taste of what later becomes apparent as the sad (and oftentimes comic) limitations of Hirshl's rebellion against his mother. Hirshl may feel the desire to contradict Tsirl and even to live a life independent of her authority, but his ability to do so is expressed so meekly that it is not sufficient to make any real difference. Even the *way* in which Hirshl tries to undermine his mother in that first scene, i.e., through a childish prank, is indicative of the type of inoffensive method Hirshl uses in order to rebel. The inevitable consequence is that by being inoffensive, Hirshl ends up being ineffectual. Alas, his mother is too tough a character to be thwarted through childish ruses.

If one looks closely at the novel, it is not difficult, however, to see how Blume could be charmed by the young Hirshl Hurvitz. In contrast to his mother's cold demeanor,[7] Hirshl is warm and effusive.[8] His way of welcoming Blume into the Hurvitz home, though done indirectly through his persistent praise of her cakes, reflects a generosity of spirit and a kindness to one obviously less fortunate than he.[9] Even the childish prank he plays on his mother discloses a clever wit on his part, as well as a willingness (albeit a meek one) to contradict falseness and hypocrisy.

Hirshl's potential as a hero, however, has trouble taking flight, for he is constantly being pulled down by his mother's devious maneuverings, many of which are done behind the scenes. And every time Hirshl manages to make an independent move away from her, she tugs even harder on the strings.

But this does not mean that Hirshl does not *try* to break free of his mother's skillfully laid-on yoke. Hirshl's budding friendship with Blume is a big step toward independence, for after all the son of a rich householder does not generally fraternize with the hired help. In fact, Hirshl, unlike his parents, does not treat Blume at all like a servant; he lends Blume books to read (18 [3:68]), which not only links them together as equals, but the books provide Blume with a cherished link to that higher realm (what we might call the aristocracy of the spirit) to which she, by all rights, should belong.[10] As the novel simply but poignantly describes her feeling for the world of books: "Blume liked books: they opened up worlds for her and reminded her of the distant days when she had sat with her father, might his soul rest in peace, reading aloud with him" (18 [3:68]).

But even within the world of books, Tsirl has been able to control (and nearly stifle) her son's intellectual potential. For example, the reader is told early in the novel that Hirshl was bright enough to even earn a doctorate (15 [3:66]). But Tsirl, fearful that the academic life would lead to madness,[11] as it ostensibly did in her brother's case, cleverly made sure Hirshl never took that route by diverting him from schooling so completely that he never even attended high school.[12] She achieved this through gradually getting Hirshl so immersed in working at the family store that he never pursued any further schooling or formal study. Consequently, it should come as no surprise to the reader that despite Hirshl's interest in books and new ideas, he basically remains an intellectual lightweight, never living up to his potential here either. The author subtly points to this fact by including a short description of the type of books he borrows from the library: one book for serious reading and *two* for light reading (18[3:68], emphasis added).

The question thus remains: what is lacking in Hirshl that prevents him from fulfilling his potential as hero and claiming his identity as his own? Is it solely his mother's fault that he is incapable of pursuing his own goals and acting on his own desires? Although his mother is indisputably one of the main obstacles in his path to independence, it is not Tsirl alone who is to blame for Hirshl's inability to act decisively. There are in fact numerous instances in the novel where Hirshl betrays a paradoxical blend of inner strength and outer cowardice that cannot be blamed directly on his mother but seems to be part of a larger complex of psychological factors at work. In such scenes, Hirshl expresses free and even radically unconventional thoughts that one might expect would lead him to independent action. But again and again, Hirshl's ideas never go beyond the unfettered world of his own mind, thus frustrating the reader's expectations. Moreover, as the disparity between thought and action continues to grow, Hirshl's psychological state becomes increasingly fragile, eventually leading him to a point of desperation that finally translates itself into "madness."[13]

An important clue to understanding the psychological barriers preventing Hirshl from fulfilling his potential as hero can be found in chapter 5. Indeed, this is one of the key chapters in the novel, for it is here that Hirshl and Blume attempt to pledge their affection for one another. Several times in this chapter Hirshl and Blume find themselves alone together, but every time that a move is made by Hirshl to hold Blume's hand or speak the appropriate words of love, it is done with such a large amount of awkwardness and embarrassment that the gesture is never completed. Twice Blume leaves the room, as if she cannot bear the discomfort of these would-be encounters (30, 33 [3:82, 3:98]). But the last time that she leaves, she returns to find Hirshl lying despondent on her bed, and she makes the bold move of stroking Hirshl's head; this time, however, it is Hirshl who gets up and leaves the room.

This waffling back and forth between affection and rejection is not only disconcerting to the reader but is puzzling as well, for the chapter had begun with an intimate glimpse of what lies in Hirshl's heart: his ceaseless thoughts of Blume and his "eyes for her alone" (27 [3:76]). Therefore, we are led to expect that once Hirshl is alone with her this will surely be the moment for him to express his feelings towards her in some decisive way. But what should have been the scene where a vow of affection is declared, or a meaningful look or touch is exchanged, instead becomes a pathetically blundered incident, an event fraught with doubt, fear, and confusion.

The hapless encounter between Hirshl and Blume, and their failure to seize the opportunity to declare their affection, should not entirely surprise the reader. If we read the early part of the chapter carefully, we discover that Agnon not only describes

Hirshl's love for Blume, but also includes a depiction of Hirshl's previous experience of women, a tale that is a mixture of passionate desire and an equally passionate *fear* of that desire (27-29 [3:96-8]). We are told that the reason for this intense fear stems partly from Hirshl's religious schooling, whose ascetic teachings had a lasting influence upon the sensitive boy, to the point that whenever he was tempted to look at a woman, he was compelled to look away.

At the same time, the narrator of the novel questions why Hirshl should hold himself to such a high standard of conduct, since "a young shopkeeper in Szybusz was not a Talmudic sage of yore" (29 [3:78]). The narrator clearly senses the humor in this unlikely parallel, and in displaying it to the reader implicitly brings out a basic inconsistency in Hirshl's psychology—Hirshl bears the conscience of a man of strict religiosity, but lives a life basically divorced from religious piety.

Indeed, it is this religious incongruity that helps to explain Hirshl's conflicting impulses toward women, and in the process sheds light on his erratic behavior toward Blume. Hirshl's strictly pious education groomed him for a religious life that scarcely existed in Szybusz anymore. Religious ideals that once were, had now given way to economic goals, so that a life lived out as the owner of a successful shop was as elevated as a rabbi's life—or better! In this environment of economic zeal, all the seductions of the modern world paraded themselves daily before Hirshl's eyes; yet his religious training sounded a loud "no" in his ears. Consequently, when it came to Blume, it is understandable that any attempt to express his love for her would be a radical step for Hirshl, who had never allowed himself the pleasure of even looking at a woman, not to mention uttering words of love.[14] It is no wonder, then, that his attempt at declaring his love to Blume turned into such a jumble of frustrated intentions and misconstrued actions. Hirshl's painful failure as a lover in this scene not only reveals his inexperience with women, but also reflects the opposing forces of desire and negation at war within his own soul.

Why, however, was Hirshl unable to simply rid himself of the "obsolete" religious restrictions, as many of the other young men of Szybusz were wont to do? The narrator gives the reader a clue to this dilemma by concluding that Hirshl's restrained behavior toward women was highly motivated by his fear of social disgrace (29 [3:78]), implying that the pursuit of women would bring shame upon him in the eyes of the people of Szybusz.[15] But why would Hirshl, of all people, be so concerned about maintaining a perfect social profile? This should not entirely surprise us if we take note of the references in the novel that tell us that the Hurvitz family regarded themselves as belonging to the bourgeois elite of the town. Their son Hirshl, therefore, was raised to share the responsibility for maintaining a high degree of middle-class respectability. It is explicitly stated that despite Hirshl's aching desire to partake of the company of women, as did many of the other young men of the town, he was unable to do so because "[t]he good breeding he had received at home was not easily overcome" (29 [3:77]).[16] The reader of course knows that in the case of the Hurvitz family this "good breeding" is a shallow pretense of superiority that has no real virtue attached to it. In fact, it serves as a debilitating force in the psychological makeup of Hirshl Hurvitz, who naively allows this societal snobbery to determine his behavior despite the unsettling fact that it is also one of the key sources of his relentless suffering.

It should be noted, however, that Hirshl's failure with Blume derives not only from his double fear of divine punishment and social disgrace, but also from the fact that Hirshl's expectations of women and their role in a romantic relationship are completely out of sync with the norms of traditional courtship. This emerges clearly at the point when a match is being planned between himself and Mina Ziemlich, and Hirshl completely fails to comprehend why Blume withdraws from him. Instead of seeing that Blume's female pride and modesty would compel her to retreat, Hirshl becomes resentful toward Blume and blames *her* for his own reluctance to oppose the match with Mina (51 [3:99]). Indeed, when Blume leaves the Hurvitz household and finds employment with the Mazals, Hirshl is filled with anger at her "rejection" of him, never considering that her leaving was a result of his weak acquiescence to the match with Mina. Later, Hirshl entertains a fantasy that Blume confides her love for him to Mrs. Mazal (which in reality she does not), and is certain that Blume will realize that she

"had to take the first step" (50 [3:98]) and return to him. The expectation that Blume will take the initiative in the romance is not
only an unlikely event in terms of her generally modest behavior
thus far; more importantly, it is a reflection of Hirshl's own misguided ideas about women, notions that have completely reversed
the traditional male-female roles in romantic pursuit. Instead of
fulfilling his role as a male,[17] which would mean aggressively pursuing the female until she is conquered, Hirshl wants Blume to take
on that part: Blume should take the initiative, and Blume should
make the first move. Of course, the tragedy is that Blume did not
expect Hirshl to slay dragons for her. He could have changed the
course of events by simply giving Blume an indication that it was
she whom he preferred. But for Hirshl to make such a move would
have been a bold step indeed, and in his mind, perhaps, just as
difficult as meeting that proverbial dragon head-on.

It is not difficult to see where Hirshl derives such inverted notions of women, for the one woman in his life that he knows well
(although perhaps not well enough)[18] is every bit the
aggressor—his mother Tsirl. Hirshl, being an only child with no
sisters, would surely look to his mother for his understanding of
women, and what he would find for his model would be a woman
who always takes the initiative with men to the point of controlling
them thoroughly. In fact the marriage of Tsirl and Boruch Meir
Hurvitz is a perfect example of an inverted role relationship where
Tsirl takes on the man's role of family decision-maker, while
Boruch Meir is like a passive receptor, affirming all her judgments.
As the novel states plainly, "Boruch Meir was not in the habit of
contradicting his wife. Sometimes he would simply repeat what she
said and sometimes he would add a few words of confirmation" (44
[3:92]).

In fact, if Hirshl was to look to his parents for an example of a
love relationship, he would certainly not find it, for theirs was
more akin to a successful business merger than a marriage of romantic desire and affection. This, however, is never stated directly
in the novel, for the narrator allows the reader to judge for himself
how truly happy such a couple could be.[19] This is skillfully
achieved at one crucial point in the novel when through the use of
ironic contrast, the narrator paints a portrait of Tsirl and Boruch

Meir alone in their store at night counting their piles of coins, while outside their window ardent young lovers are courting in the evening's shadows:

> Could there be a greater pleasure in life than sitting at night in one's store with one's profits laid out before one? Schilling rose above schilling on the counter, and all was right with the world.
>
> Out in the street the young couples went by and sometimes even dropped to their knees. Ah, how many more long nights of courting like these did they still have ahead of them, nor was the outcome sure even then! Meanwhile one sat with one's wife in one's store amid a fragrance of cinnamon, figs, and raisins. A last parting trace of the warmth of the sun lingered on in these fruits, which retained it even dried and packed in crates.
>
> Silently Tsirl and Boruch Meir sat listening. What could they be straining to hear? A line of a song sung in faraway climes by the planters of such southern vines and trees? The last echo of a kiss that a shepherd gave his love beneath them? . . . .
>
> Tsirl and Boruch Meir, in any event, had no time for such diversions. Boruch Meir never pretended to be Tsirl's lover, and Tsirl never drove Boruch Meir out of his senses. He simply was as happy with her as she was with him. Their days passed in the making of money, and if now and then they chose to rest from it, they generally did so in silence. (43 [3:91-2])

This "happy" portrait of Tsirl and Boruch Meir is meaningfully cast in a pseudo-romantic light (the "fragrance of cinnamon" etc.) for in a bizarre sense, they do share a kind of fevered excitement in their relationship that is strangely close to that of romantic desire—but, in their case, it is their shared love of money that unites them, rather than love. At the same time, the juxtaposition of Tsirl and Boruch in their store counting their profits with that of young lovers sighing beneath their windowpane delivers such an ironic punch that it makes it hard to miss the fact that their relationship is so far from anything akin to true romantic love that to even draw the comparison verges on the grotesque.

As for Hirshl himself, his relationship with his mother is unlikely to teach him much about affection, for Tsirl's lack of tenderness toward her son is evident almost from the beginning of the novel. Although the narrator tells us little about Hirshl's early years, we are informed of a few salient details, such as the fact that Tsirl returned to work in the store as soon as Hirshl was weaned (10 [3:62]). Although this may not be shocking to contemporary readers, this would surely not have been a common practice among middle-class women at the turn of the century when this story was set, and would have likely signaled to the reader a disturbing lack of natural maternal affection.[20] Another significant detail that is also included in the novel is the fact that Tsirl never sang Hirshl any lullabies when he was a small child (190 [3:233]), again communicating to the reader that Tsirl is deficient in those basic motherly qualities of tenderness and affection.[21] It is not difficult to deduce from these small but pointed details that Hirshl suffers from a kind of emotional neglect at the hands of his mother. In light of this, Hirshl's erratic behavior with Blume becomes quite understandable, especially after one realizes that it is very likely that Hirshl would be unsure whether his own mother truly loves him. Indeed, it is this extreme emotional fragility which may largely account for Hirshl's inability to confidently express his feelings of love for Blume, and which may also go far to explain why Hirshl becomes quickly convinced of Blume's rejection of him, even when this presumption is entirely unwarranted.[22]

At the same time, it is not only Tsirl's lack of affection that makes Hirshl susceptible to self-doubt, but Tsirl actively does her part to reinforce Hirshl's fear of rejection. This is revealed clearly in her speech to him after Blume leaves their household, "No one chooses his own fate. Better to marry a woman who respects you than to run after one who doesn't care" (51 [3:100]). These words, of course, confirm all of Hirshl's worst fears about Blume, i.e., that she left their home because she did not care for him. Moreover, it is implied that if he should try to pursue her he would not only make a fool of himself, but he would be undertaking a hopeless task, for he would be trying to challenge fate itself.

This pretense of wisdom on Tsirl's part about her son's destiny is clearly an essential part of her control over Hirshl. This may be obvious to the reader, but it is certainly not apparent to Hirshl, who trusts his mother's "prophetic" judgments, not seeing that they may well be calculated to engineer his fate rather than predict it. In fact it is precisely at such moments of weakness and despair that Hirshl falls prey to Tsirl's exclusive control, causing him to give up any notions of independent action. This may be because these are the only times that Tsirl displays any affection for her son. Note how Hirshl expresses a sudden feeling of extreme closeness to his mother after Blume "rejects him," and how he recalls another such moment from his childhood:

> Indeed, just being near his mother made Hirshl dewy-eyed these days. As distant as he had felt from her, there was now no one in the world who seemed closer to him. Once, when he had been a small boy, a friend had jilted him; seeing how hurt he was Tsirl took him in her arms, where her kisses and caresses soon put the friend out of his mind. And although Hirshl was now a young man, the same thing had happened again. (52 [3:100])

The fact that this is the only mention in the novel of Tsirl expressing tender feelings for Hirshl is significant in itself, for it shows that Tsirl knows *how* to express motherly affection, but she only does so if it suits her purposes. In fact the novel subtly reveals how such a mother-son relationship begins its sinister course. Under normal circumstances, Tsirl conveys little affection for her son. But when Hirshl is hurt by another, Tsirl quickly moves in to fill the void and makes it seem as if she is the only one who truly cares for him. This, of course, renders Hirshl completely dependent on her for love. However, like a miser who delights in another man's want, Tsirl continues to withhold her love from Hirshl, and only offers it when he comes to her thoroughly alone and dejected. One could even speculate that in an unconscious way Hirshl seeks out rejection, for it is only then that he receives a sure display of affection from his mother, almost like a reward for learning his lesson that surely no one could ever love him as much as she.

If this is indeed the case, that Tsirl wants to maintain exclusive control over her son, why would she be bent on matching him with Mina Ziemlich? Would not Tsirl be equally threatened by Mina as she had obviously been by Bluma, who jeopardized her monopoly on Hirshl's affections? [23] The answer is clearly no: Tsirl would not be threatened by Mina in the least, because Tsirl saw that Hirshl did not care for her,[24] and therefore he would be unlikely to stray from his usual obeisance to his mother's will. In other words, Hirshl would still belong to Tsirl, heart and soul. In Tsirl's eyes, a marriage of convenience rather than a marriage of love would therefore be the preferred arrangement, not only because of its obvious material advantages, but because it would guarantee Hirshl's primary loyalty to his mother unendingly.[25]

Hirshl's response to his mother's plan for his future is not a simple one. Indeed, it is here that we see a clear indication of the gap between Hirshl's thoughts and actions starting to widen. In other words, he begins the process of a weak-minded retreat into his own thoughts as his only form of resistance. Thus, although Hirshl formally acquiesces in the match with Mina Ziemlich, he does not completely accept the idea of their impending marriage within his own mind. In fact, the idea of "escape" begins to take root in Hirshl's consciousness on the very eve of their engagement. It is also here that Hirshl begins to think about his notoriously mad uncle who ran off to the woods, and he wonders whether "he wasn't crazy after all," but "knew what he was doing" (64 [3:112]). Hirshl clearly begins to identify with his uncle, and seems to implicitly wonder if his uncle too had been caught in a similarly untenable position, and merely acted mad in order to escape his situation.

Hirshl continues to contemplate escape the morning after his engagement to Mina and even dreams of running off to America. But at the same time, Hirshl admits to himself that he would never actually do anything of that sort because of his being an only child, implying that the consequent pain it would bring to his parents would make such an act unthinkable. He merely enjoyed the fantasy of escape because "imagining it kept him from despair" (69 [3:118]). The narrator, however, lets the reader know that it is not only Hirshl's concern for his parents' feelings that prevents him from doing something courageous like running off to America. This in fact seems to be more an excuse for inaction than an honest reason. The truth is that Hirshl is himself not fit for such tough action, partly because he is overly attached to the soft comforts of home and hearth in Szybusz. As the narrator ironically describes the syndrome:

> And if something as insubstantial as air could keep a man
> from leaving Szybusz, a weightier substance like a blanket or
> a pillow had an even more powerful effect. No matter how of-
> ten Hirshl thought of running away, each time he laid his head
> on his pillow and pulled his blanket up over him he knew that
> he would never go anywhere. (71 [3:119])

As this passage so humorously portrays, Hirshl is completely un-
fit for a bold act like fleeing the country. As the pampered son of a
Jewish bourgeois family, he thoroughly lacks the ruggedness and
determination that is needed for strong action. An escape to America would mean hardship, deprivation, and struggle, experiences
that boys like Hirshl had been shielded from all their lives. For Hirshl to overcome such a soft upbringing and take a step in a new direction, he would need to turn his back on all his habitual comforts,
something Hirshl clearly was unwilling or unable to do.

Hirshl nevertheless stubbornly clings to the idea of freeing himself from marrying Mina. During the engagement dinner at the
Ziemlich home, Hirshl plans in his mind to rid himself of Mina
once and for all by insulting her to her face, and thus presumably
making himself so repellant to her that she would break the engagement. But as usual, Hirshl's inner life has little influence on his actual behavior. Being "too much of a gentleman" to go through with
it (75 3:123]), he instead sits and talks with her, so much in fact
that his words come pouring out of him "in a torrent of uncon-
trolled speech."

However, when Tsirl smilingly enters the room in which they
are conversing, Hirshl feels resentful that she's ruining his "good
time" (76 [3:125]), and he grabs Mina's hand as if it "were his only
support in the world." This strange action on Hirshl's part seems
perplexing at first, because the reader knows that Hirshl is not terribly enamored of Mina. Also, why would Hirshl think Tsirl is
trying to ruin his time with Mina when he knows that it is Tsirl
who has been promoting the match from the beginning? If one pon-
ders this carefully, one realizes that the inclusion of these details is
proof of Agnon's clear understanding of the odd workings of a repressed psychology such as Hirshl's. It in fact becomes evident
that Hirshl's inappropriate reaction to Tsirl in this situation is a
manifestation of the bottled-up anger he feels toward her, and es-

pecially toward her interference in matters of the heart. In actuality, Hirshl is still filled with resentment toward his mother for having come between him and Blume, and for contriving this new match with Mina. But his is a displaced resentment toward Tsirl that comes out in the wrong place at the wrong time: he should have been angry with his mother a few weeks ago over the issue of Blume; instead his anger emerges now in defense of a woman he does not even care for. His grabbing hold of Mina's hand in front of his mother can thus be understood as an act of defiance, almost as if Mina *is* Blume. To the reader, however, this misplaced attempt at manliness is also comic (though pathetically so), for here we have Hirshl defending his right to the very woman his mother is forcing on him, and by doing so he falls further and further into Tsirl's trap.

The growing sense in the novel that Hirshl is being "trapped" is an idea that begins to take root unconsciously even in the minds of others at the Ziemlich dinner party. When Hirshl is greeted by the matchmaker Yona Toyber as they enter the dining room, Hirshl's father notices that Toyber uses a familiar line from a joke about a hangman who says to the condemned man, "What, you too are here?" But Boruch Meir is in such a jovial mood that he does not even think about the fact that the comparison between Hirshl and a man about to be hanged is "not auspicious" (77 [3:125]). The reader, however, gets the hint: it is at this dinner where Hirshl's fate is being sealed, and like a man being led to the gallows, Hirshl is trapped on a road of no return.

Although Boruch Meir does not take Toyber's joke seriously, certainly Hirshl unconsciously feels the weight of it, for it is here at the Ziemlich engagement dinner that we witness the beginning of Hirshl's internal rebellion against the type of bourgeois life in which a marriage to Mina would entrap him. But this rebellion does not take the form of a protest against his parents or Mina. Instead, Hirshl expresses his rebellion by what he does *not* do: he barely eats any of the food set out before him, and in his mind he silently condemns the lavish fare, particularly the meat, calling it "cooked dead flesh" and "abominations"[26] (80 [3:128]). It is almost as if he were imagining himself a prophet condemning the licentious behavior of the crude multitude, which is of course a humorously incongruous role for one as passive as he.

The extent to which Hirshl feels himself an "outsider" at this event is made clear by the fact that Hirshl returns to thinking about his late uncle. Just as he had speculated on the eve of his engagement to Mina, Hirshl again questions whether his uncle was truly mad, pondering whether he "might not have been a misunderstood vegetarian who took to the woods to lead a healthier life" (80 [3:128]). Note that there seems to be a pattern of identification developing between Hirshl and his mad uncle, for Hirshl starts to construe a new image of his uncle as a man in a situation similar to his own—that is, not as someone truly mad, but as someone merely "misunderstood" or alienated from the mainstream of society. In fact, the reader begins to see that as Hirshl feels increasingly trapped in a loveless relationship, his dissatisfaction manifests itself as a kind of psychological *separateness* not only from Mina but from the rest of society. This feeling of separateness leads Hirshl to speculate that perhaps madness is not the result of a curse or an illness, but is merely the state of being *different* in a society in which conformity is the ruling passion.

Although Hirshl's rejection of food at the Ziemlichs' dinner party begins on a sure footing, he does not maintain this "rebellious" stance for long. The enticing aroma of the food gets the better of him, and he ends up devouring a large slice of cornmeal pudding. Although Hirshl berates himself for "being a pig like the rest of them" (81 [3:129]), this is not the thing that humiliates him the most. What truly wounds him to the core is his mother's perfectly chosen remark to him as he eats the pudding, "'You must admit, Hirshl,' said Tsirl, flashing him a smile, 'that this pudding is delicious'" (81 [3:129]). Hirshl immediately recognizes these words as the same as those that he uttered to Tsirl on the morning he first met Blume in their home. The significance of these words is twofold: not only do they bring back the painful memory of his love for Blume and his loss of her; but more importantly, these are also the identical words that Hirshl had used *against* Tsirl in what had been an incipient attempt to rebel against her and expose her hypocrisy.[27] Now, in what could be seen as an act of vengeance, Tsirl recalls these same words and throws them back at Hirshl as a kind of declaration of victory over him, for she has succeeded in quashing his rebellion and in bringing him this far along in her plan. But Tsirl never' betrays her thirst for vengeance, and therefore speaks the words with a smile on her face. And certainly Tsirl has much to smile about: she has taken Hirshl away from Blume and betrothed him to Mina, all without protestation or confrontation. In fact, with these lines spoken by Tsirl, the novel has come full circle and reversed itself, for unlike in chapter 1, it is now Tsirl who is the victor and Hirshl who is the vanquished one. And so ends this portion of Hirshl's youth, for gone is the possibility of Hirshl's independence, and gone is Blume who first inspired Hirshl with that possibility. Together they have all but vanished from sight.[28]

Notes

1. Gershon Shaked similarly refers to the failure of love in the novel as a "sikui she-huhmatz" (literally, an opportunity that has gone sour). See Gershon Shaked, *Panim aherot be-yetsirato shel Shai 'Agnon* (Tel Aviv: Hakibbutz Hameuchad, 1989), 69.

2. David Aberbach says that from a psychological viewpoint, *Sipur pashut* is "Agnon's central work." See David Aberbach, *At the Handles of the Lock* (New York: Oxford University Press, 1984), 162.

3. I believe that Hirshl fits more closely into the tradition of the mock hero than he does the anti-hero. To be an anti-hero would imply that he *is* a hero but of a new type. In my reading of the novel, Hirshl is not a hero at present, but had merely the potential to be one, but failed. For a discussion of the hero in literature see the collection of essays compiled and edited by Victor Brombert, *The Hero in Literature* (Greenwich, Conn.: Fawcett, 1969).

4. A good example of his inflated idea of himself (that has nothing to do with reality!) occurs on p. 47 [3:95]: "Even though he had not talked back to his mother, he felt quite heroic. But Blume had disappeared. . . . How he had fought for her, and here she was looking right through him!" Here Hirshl believes that he fought for Blume, even though the reader knows that he did no such thing. All he did was be silent when his mother proposed a match between himself and Mina Ziemlich.

5. In his astute study of Agnon's work, David Aberbach traces many of Hirshl's problems back to his faulty relationship with his mother, a relationship that keeps him in a perpetual state of childish dependence and suppressed anger. Although I think that this is indeed a crucial part of Hirshl's psychology, I do not think that it completely accounts for Hirshl's failed relationship with Blume. In my view, the psychoanalytic approach that Aberbach takes (although he claims it is not strictly so) is very useful for understanding aspects of character, but has its limitations in that it tends to fit everything into a preconceived formula. See David Aberbach, *At the Handles of the Lock* (London: Oxford, 1984).

6. Baruch Kurzweil also interprets these words of praise for Bluma's cakes to be highly significant, and considers them to be the first expression of Hirshl's love for Bluma. See Baruch Kurzweil, *Masot 'al sipure Shai 'Agnon* (Jerusalem: Schocken, 1970), 357.

7. Even though Tsirl has appeared only briefly thus far in the novel, it is easy to perceive the coldness of her character, especially expressed in her facial movements: her pursed lips, etc. For a discussion of the significance of gestures and movements of the body in the work of Agnon, see the book by Dov Landau, *Mi-signon le-mashma'ut besipure Shai 'Agnon* (Tel Aviv, Israel: Eked, 1988), especially chapter 5, 126-44.

8. Note that this is true of Hirshl at the beginning of the novel, but becomes less so as it progresses, as we shall discuss later on.

9. Hirshl's sensitivity towards others seems to be an important trait that the author is trying to stress, since the chapter significantly ends on this very point

(10 [3:61]). Note also, however, that the discussion of his sensitivity is ironically undermined by what I have previously called "the voice of Szybusz" that dismisses it and says that maybe he was just a boy with an impractical turn of mind, i.e., it's just an immature phase that he'll outgrow.

10. See my previous chapter on this point—Blume as unrecognized princess. Note that Dov Sadan in his article "Sipur 'al *Sipur pashut*" also conceives of Blume in similar terms, saying, "ve-har-e Bluma she-hi hativa shel atzilut mutzna'at" (38). Dov Sadan, *'Al Shai 'Agnon* (Tel Aviv, Israel: Hakibbutz Hameuchad, 1978), 36-40.

11. Note that it is uncertain in the novel whether Tsirl's brother had truly gone mad, or whether he had merely been perceived as such by a society that could not understand intellectuals or those with new ideas.

12. The fact that Hirshl never attended high school is made clear in the original Hebrew ([3:66]), but gets lost in Halkin's English translation of the novel.

13. It is debatable whether Hirshl truly went mad, or was merely in desperate need of a temporary escape from his interminably boring wife and mind-numbing job in his parents' shop. The question of Hirshl's madness will be discussed at greater length in the next chapter.

14. Hirshl's cautious attitude toward women should not entirely surprise the reader, given the historical context. Although the popularization of the idea of romantic love had taken hold in European society by the nineteenth century (inspired by the rise of Enlightenment ideas and the subsequent European Romantic movement), the traditional Jewish communities of Eastern Europe approached the idea of romantic love with suspicion, and clung to the institution of the arranged marriage as long as they could. In fact, one of the major innovations of the Haskalah (Enlightenment) was the right to choose one's own mate based on love, a notion that gradually displaced the traditional practice of the arranged marriage. See Jacob Katz, *Tradition and Crisis: Jewish Society at the End of the Middle Ages* (New York: Schocken, 1961), 142-44, 268-9. Cf. also David Biale, "Eros and Enlightenment" in *Eros and the Jews* (New York: Basic Books, 1992), 149-75.

15. Note that the translator uses the word "prudence" twice in this chapter to explain Hirshl's wisdom that prevented him from bringing shame upon himself, in case he were to give in to his desires. In the original Hebrew of *Sipur pashut*, the word *bina* is used in the first context (27 [3:76]) and then *sekhel* in the second (29 [3:78]), both of which Halkin translates as "prudence"—a good choice, in my opinion, for it implies practical intelligence.

16. Note the resemblance here to Thomas Mann's novel *Buddenbrooks*, wherein the heroine Tony's inbred sense of her family's prominent social position (successful merchants, like the Hurvitz family) causes her to reject the young man she loves, and marry one befitting her "station"—with disastrous results.

17. There are numerous ideologically-based works that in recent years have been written (mostly feminist in origin) that attempt to deny that there are such things as intrinsically male and female behavioral roles. Although I do not wish to debate the point within this limited space, I believe that one can justifiably

conclude that one should read literature in terms of the time it was written, and hence avoid what I'would deem to be the all-too-common mistake of reading into it ideas from a later time that clearly do not apply. Therefore, when I speak of Hirshl's role as a male, I mean it in the traditional sense in which it was understood at the time when Agnon was writing. For a discussion of this principle of reading, see E. D. Hirsch, Jr., *Validity in Interpretation* (New Haven, Conn.: Yale University Press, 1967), 40-44, 245-64. Cf. also Robert Alter, *The Pleasures of Reading in an Ideological Age* (New York: Simon and Schuster, 1989), 221-28.

18. I think it can be argued that part of Hirshl's problem is the fact that he does not see the full extent of his mother's cunning and manipulative character. This is not entirely Hirshl's fault, for Tsirl is extremely adept at masking her deeds and intentions. For a good example of this, see how she deftly manages to make it seem as if the decision about the match between Hirshl and Mina was done in consultation with her husband, whereas she had single-handedly arranged (or masterminded) it with the matchmaker, prior to any discussion with Boruch Meir (44-5 [3:92-4]).

19. This literary technique, which allows the reader to draw his own conclusions from the dissonant facts, is one that Robert Alter traces back to writers such as Flaubert and (in a qualified sense) to midrashic narrative. See Alter's excellent chapter on Agnon's literary technique, entitled "Agnon's Psychological Realism," in Robert Alter, *Hebrew and Modernity* (Bloomington: Indiana University Press, 1994), 134-53.

20. I think it is fair to say that even when this novel was published in 1935, this would have been a rather unusual practice for a middle-class Jewish woman in towns like Szybusz.

21. Note the thematic resemblance here to the story by Mendele Mocher Seforim, "Dos Tosefos-Yom-Tov kelbel" (1910), contained in his *Sefer habehemot*, and translated into English as "The Calf" in *A Treasury of Yiddish Stories*, eds. Irving Howe and Eliezer Greenberg (New York: Schocken, 1973), 97-111. This story depicts the emotional starvation of a young boy who suffers neglect at the hands of his mother. In Mendele's story, however, there is some economic justification to account for why the mother is so heartless—she is a poor widow with many young children to care for, who must occupy most of her time dealing with the harsh practicalities of life. In contrast, the Agnon novel portrays a well-off Jewish mother who has little excuse for her emotional neglect of her only child.

22. For some examples of the way in which Hirshl's thoughts progressed to the point where he was convinced of Blume's rejection of him, see p. 47 ([3:95]): "As dearly as he loved Blume, not only was she giving him no encouragement, she was actually spurning him." See also p. 51 ([3:99]): "It puzzled Hirshl why he was not angrier with Mina for coming between him and Blume. Dimly he felt that not she but Blume was to blame, since if Blume had been nicer to him, there would have been no question of Mina." Note also the resemblance here to Agnon's later story, "Ha-rofe u-gerushato" (1941), in which the doctor becomes neurotically convinced of his wife's betrayal of him even though his suspicions had nothing to do with reality.

23. Note that I use the word "monopoly" intentionally here, because I think Tsirl treats Hirshl much in the same way she does her material acquisitions, i.e., with completely selfish motives and a total disregard for anyone but herself. Hirshl's feelings were clearly treated with a similar disregard by his mother.

24. In his article on *Sipur pashut,* A. B. Yehoshua suggests that Tsirl's motives in matching Hirshl with Mina are deeply rooted in a kind of primitive oedipal rivalry. As Yehoshua puts it: "Tsirl immediately notices the motherly essence in Blume that attracts Hirshl, and deeply fearing that Blume will absorb all the eros of her son, she makes sure to send her away, and to find a completely different sort of woman to be his wife—a child-woman who cannot provide Hirshl with the motherly essence that he so lacks; thus she will not constitute a threat to the ties between Tsirl and her son." See A. B. Yehoshua, "Plot and Denouement in *Sipur pashut,*" in *Agnon: Texts and Contexts in English Translation,* ed. Leon I. Yudkin (New York: Markus Wiener, 1988), 149-50.

25. Note how the narrator describes Tsirl's relief at Hirshl's engagement to Mina: "Indeed, how can we have mentioned Tsirl so often without having mentioned her eyes? Although she had only two of them, their power was great—and never so much as now that she kept them fixed on Boruch Meir while never taking them off Mina, for whom she felt a special affection for having agreed to become her daughter-in-law, thus saving Hirshl from the clutches of Blume" (62-3 [3:111]).

26. See my discussion of the great significance of food to the people of Szybusz in chapter 2, above, 49-51.

27. See my discussion above, 58-9. Note that Nitza Ben-Dov also interprets this scene with the cake as bearing special significance. She regards it as symbolically revealing the ongoing rivalry in Tsirl's mind between herself and Blume for Hirshl's affection. Thus, according to Ben-Dov, Hirshl's eating of the cake is proof to Tsirl that Hirshl has "betrayed his love for Blume." Although I essentially agree with this reading, I think it overemphasizes Tsirl's oedipal impulses toward her son, explaining her in purely Freudian terms, and thereby reducing the complexity of her character. See Nitza Ben-Dov, *Agnon's Art of Indirection* (Leiden, The Netherlands: E. J. Brill, 1993), 77-9.

28. Note that after Blume leaves the Hurvitz home, she also departs from the plot, never to reemerge again in any decisive way. Interestingly, she is mentioned at one point in Agnon's later novel *Ore'ah nata lalun* (1939). In this work, the narrator asks in a rhetorical fashion about Blume's fate. The answer he then gives is highly elusive, stating only that her story could fill a book, and goes on to say that God only knows when it will be written. See *Kol sipurav shel Shmuel Yosef 'Agnon,* second edition, vol. 4, *Ore'ah nata lalun* (Tel Aviv, Israel: Schocken, 1953), 308. For some further comments on Blume's fate, see note 30 in chapter 5 below.

Chapter 4

Agnon the Psychologist (Part 2):
The Sorrows of Young Hirshl—
Madness As the Weak Man's Escape
from Unhappiness

The fact that love is denied a place in the life of our young Jewish hero Hirshl Hurvitz is a reality that becomes increasingly unsettling to the reader as the novel progresses, especially since the author has already chosen to give us several glimpses into the romantic nature of Hirshl's soul. We have been witness to Hirshl's profound feelings of affection for Blume Nacht which, despite his tender years, are certainly no passing whim or infatuation. To Hirshl, Blume is so closely linked to him that she is repeatedly said to be like his "twin" (27, 50 [3:76, 98]). His attempts at erasing her from his heart and mind can never truly convince the reader, and soon enough do not even serve to convince himself. Our hero is like a prince in a fairy story who has sworn his love to a fair maiden: nothing can supplant his avowed love—neither comforts nor honor, and certainly not marriage to another.

It should then come as no surprise to the reader that the wedding of Hirshl to a woman other than Blume, Mina Ziemlich, features a bride and groom who are present in body but not in spirit. At the wedding ceremony Hirshl is described as looking "wan and tired," and Mina "as pale as a tallow candle" (105 [3:151]).[1] One perceptive guest draws the appropriate conclusion from their lifeless appearance, and remarks: "'It's God's truth,' said Hayyim Yehoshua, 'that the groom doesn't look like a groom to me.' 'And the bride?' asked Mottshi Shaynbart. 'The same goes for the bride'" (104 [3:150-51]). To everyone else at the event, however, it is a gay affair full of all the usual sentiment and hoopla. But Hirshl and Mina are strangely detached from the whirl of festivities surrounding them, and wonder what all the fuss is about. Note how Mina's impassive state of mind is depicted: "Mina sat by Hirshl's side wondering why such a great to-do was made about love. Not that she had anything against Hirshl. Far from it. But she had been content with her life before he came along too" (106 [3:153]). The reader here realizes that it is not only Hirshl who feels no love for his bride, but Mina herself is indifferent to Hirshl as an individual. It is just that, unlike Hirshl, she contentedly accepts the match as a fact of life, and does not long for more. In fact, for Mina, this *is* love; she merely sees it as something entirely overrated.

Although Mina is emotionally withdrawn at the wedding, Hirshl's psychological state is even more strained than hers, and his mind darts distractedly from one topic to another. When one of the candles under the wedding canopy suddenly blows out, Hirshl does not even notice it, even though the narrator informs the reader that this is a bad luck omen according to Jewish folk belief. At the same time, it is perhaps no accident that Hirshl's mind flits immediately to the subject of divorce. In a bizarre leap of logic he is reminded of how he once heard that those of the Hindu faith use candles to decide on divorce settlements. Notwithstanding the humor in this ill-suited juxtaposition of marriage and divorce (not to mention the unlikely parallel of Jew and Hindu!), it is obvious to the reader that a groom who is thinking about divorce while still under the wedding canopy is not too happy about his marriage vows. In fact, it reveals that even though Hirshl is physically going through the motions of a bridegroom, he is thinking about somehow getting out of the marriage right up until the last moment. Perhaps even more significantly, Hirshl's thoughts of divorce may also serve as a consoling reminder to him that an "escape hatch" such as divorce is always there if he needs it. In other words, he can endure the marriage as long as he knows that the option of escape is always present.

In fact, Hirshl's constant thoughts of *escape* give us a vital clue into the workings of his psychology, for it explains his seeming ability to reconcile the opposing factions of thought and action. His thoughts continue to take radical twists and turns, yet his actions are those of a man slavishly devoted to an ordinary existence.[2] But like the mythic *galut* Jew who can put up with any indignity because of his belief in the coming of the messiah, Hirshl seems able to endure anything because of his persistent belief in the idea of escape.[3]

At the beginning of his married life, however, Hirshl does try to harness his thoughts and live the life of the dutiful husband in mind and body.[4] As the novel hints, this may be because as newlyweds, Hirshl and Mina are experiencing the initial excitement of their physical relationship. The reader in fact is almost persuaded that Hirshl is beginning to love Mina.[5] However, this is an illusion that is short-lived, for one soon discovers how little the couple have in common. As the narrator informs us, "If not for the hot blood of youth that they shared, there would have been nothing between them" (109 [3:156]). Hirshl nevertheless endeavors to forge an intellectual bond with Mina, as is evident in his attempt to share his interest in books with her (just as he once did with Blume). But Hirshl learns quickly that it is a pointless pursuit. As the novel tells us, "no sooner did he begin to explain than she started to yawn," so that "[i]n the end Hirshl learned to keep both his books and his knowledge to himself" (109 [3:156]).

At the same time, the author continues to delude the reader into thinking that Hirshl is slowly adjusting to his marriage to Mina. This is a narrative technique that compels the reader to be ensnared in the same type of self-deception that Hirshl is caught up in. The reader can almost be fooled into believing that Hirshl is learning to live happily according to the norms of his society, a society that views a prudent marriage to be far more important than love.

Nevertheless, Hirshl's outward appearance of contentedness is consistently undermined by the numerous subtleties included in the novel which betray his mounting unhappiness. Indeed, a close look at the early married life of Hirshl and Mina will show that as individuals there is a striking dissimilarity between the two of them that becomes increasingly evident. Even when Hirshl and Mina visit with Mina's parents in their country village for the holiday of Sukkot and are surrounded by the beauties of nature, the newlyweds' differences are only made larger. Hirshl is invigorated by the fresh air and the natural environment, and seems to feel liberated to be far away from "the narrow crooked streets of Szybusz, where each holiday booth looked like a pack on a hunchback's back" (114 [3:160]). It is clear from this comparison that life in Szybusz is associated in Hirshl's mind with all that is unnatural and deformed. But Mina, unlike Hirshl, is thrilled by the attractions of city life, and has no interest in the simple pleasures of country living. Though born in the village, Mina is restless during her visits home, and aches to get back to the excitement of the relatively urban atmosphere of Szybusz.

Another small but vital detail that similarly reveals this fundamental difference between Hirshl and Mina is made evident at the point in the novel where Hirshl sits basking in the natural splendor of the Ziemlichs' country *sukkah*. Hirshl looks up at Mina and wonders what she is doing there (115 [3:162]), which is puzzling to the reader since it is Mina's family home they are visiting. On second glance, however, Hirshl's question becomes intelligible since it seems to reflect Hirshl's feeling that Mina somehow does not fit into this robust atmosphere of natural beauty. And indeed she does not, for even though she was born in this country village, her urban schooling has trained her to become anything but a simple "country girl." As we can see from some of the details used to describe her in this scene, Mina is not only pitifully "thin and pale" (115 [3:162]), but she has no interest in simple country pleasures; indeed, she is dedicated to what would in Hirshl's eyes be mere artificial forms of beauty—her "tailored clothes" (115 [3:162]), and her cologne that she uses a little too liberally (116 [3:162]). Similarly, Hirshl's attraction to country living is incomprehensible to Mina, who seems to be doing all she can to mask her simple origins. This split between them is of course only one aspect of the larger gulf separating them, which explains the boredom and frustration, expressed hesitantly by both of them, that runs like a threatening undercurrent throughout this part of the novel. But this is not easily admitted to, even when one's entire happiness is at stake, for as the novel shows, the psychological effort to deny a harsh reality is sometimes harder to overcome than that reality itself.

Indeed, the entire psychological portrait of Hirshl Hurvitz is far from simple, especially as the reader begins to witness the early signs of his mental breakdown and eventual "madness." Consequently, his psychological unravelling does not follow a logical progression. It takes numerous twists and turns so that there are times when one is convinced that Hirshl is finding some satisfaction in his marriage,[6] and then at other times one gets the clear impression that a gnawing unhappiness is causing him to lose his inner control over his "rebellious" thoughts of dissatisfaction with his wife.[7] At a specific point in the novel, however, the strength of Hirshl's "rebellious" thoughts finally wins out over all his desperate efforts to subdue them and make the best of his mundane existence as a distracted husband in a loveless marriage. Significantly, this turning point is when Mina becomes pregnant with their first child, an event that ties Hirshl's fate to Mina more tightly than ever (chapter 19).

Hirshl now begins to withdraw from Mina in a manner that starts to become obvious even to her. Mina at first suspects that Hirshl is in love with another woman—which is actually true, except that she has the wrong person in mind. She thinks it is the "glamorous" Sophia Gildenhorn, a suspicion which reveals how little Mina knows Hirshl, for he has no interest in women of false sophistication like Sophia. This misunderstanding leads Hirshl to reveal to Mina an aspect of himself that had heretofore remained hidden: he takes the bold step of telling Mina for the first time about his mad uncle. But this ends up being less a revelation about his family's secret than it is a personal confession (and perhaps a warning), for it seems to have more to do with Hirshl's own circumstances than it does with his late uncle's.[8] He tells her that in his opinion his uncle was not mad at all, but just pretended to be crazy in order to avoid being married off to a woman he did not love. In Hirshl's words, such a marriage would have left his uncle "an empty shell of a man" (127 [3:173]), a statement that clearly reveals the way Hirshl feels about himself.

Hirshl then goes on to tell Mina about the author of a Hebrew dictionary who used a similar ruse: in order to escape a loveless marriage, he feigned madness by putting his *tefillin* on his cat; he was then easily granted a divorce by his wife's family and later married a woman of his own choice (128 [3:174]). Although the reader should be aware that Hirshl seems to be slanting these stories to make an oblique point about his own life, there is a common thread that runs through both stories that should not go unnoticed. Both are about the desperation experienced by men who are forced to marry women they do not love. They are trapped by circumstances not of their own making, and use madness as a last desperate act to escape their marriages and finally take control of their own destinies. In his uncle's case, the story ended tragically with his eventual death, whereas in the bizarre tale of the Hebraist, it ended happily with his marriage to a woman he loved. This, then, becomes Hirshl's dilemma: if he too takes the route of "madness" as his only way out of the marriage, what will be *his* fate? Will he end up like his uncle and destroy himself in the process, or will he be like the clever Hebrew author who fooled them all and ended up on top? At this point in the novel, this is a gamble that Hirshl is not yet ready to take.

Hirshl's emotional withdrawal from his wife is soon accompanied by a general distaste for other people, especially for the Gildenhorns and their "gang," who had been making a habit of congregating at Hirshl's and Mina's apartment. The narrator explains the change in Hirshl's feelings towards his guests as follows: "now that his home had lost its charm for him, so had playing host" (128 [3:174]). In other words, Hirshl's conscious dissatisfaction with Mina now begins to spill over onto his feelings toward people in general. As a result, the usual visitors who had been coming to call on the young couple now stop coming, likely sensing Hirshl's coolness toward them.

Cutting himself off from the company of others contributes further to Hirshl's psychological retreat into the world of his own thoughts, and it is at this point in the novel that Hirshl begins to think obsessively about Blume. He longs so much to see her that he is unable to think about anything else, to the point that even his mother notices that he is "out of sorts" (132 [3:178]). Pastimes in which Hirshl used to find enjoyment have now lost all their appeal, such as reading books, traveling to the country, and frequenting the

Zionist clubhouse. In fact, when Hirshl returns briefly to the club-house, he hardly participates in the social life there, preferring to sit silently by himself. It seems as if his dissatisfaction with his life and his subsequent withdrawal from people has made him unsure about his own worth as an individual. As the narrator states, "Hirshl's silence was more a matter of feeling that he was unworthy of being listened to" (134 [3:180]). Eventually Hirshl's emotional withdrawal from his old chums at the clubhouse becomes so acute that he finally ceases to go there at all.

If Hirshl's unhappiness with his marriage is so profound that it affects his entire sense of well-being, then one might ask, why does he not attempt to leave Mina and return to Blume? Certainly the reader's expectations have been sufficiently aroused that anything less would be a disappointment. Although Hirshl has thus far not behaved much like the hero in a classic romance, the structure of the story is such that it still strives for a resolution that would unite the hero with his true love. One could in fact argue that Hirshl *does* attempt to bring about such a resolution, but he does so in a way that is backhanded and ultimately unsuccessful. This is because Hirshl's actions are directed inward rather than projected outward into the world. As a hero with bravery only "of the mind," Hirshl's acts of decision are confined to his own mental world.[9] Thus, Hirshl does "leave" Mina, in the sense that he withdraws from her emotionally, perhaps hoping that she will find him so intolerable that she will actually be the one who decides to leave *him.* In a similar vein, Hirshl "returns" to Blume in the sense that he increasingly focuses all his thoughts upon her, believing that if he thinks about her hard enough she will come to him (132, 141 [3:178, 187]). Not surprisingly, none of these ploys work, mostly because they depend on someone else to take all the risks, in this case the female characters. Certainly a hero who waits for the heroine to rescue him is a reversal that is not likely to succeed.[10] Without any active attempt by the hero to free *himself* from this morass that is partly of his own making, there can be no simple resolution to this ironic tale of the lovelorn Hirshl Hurvitz.

But Agnon continues to give the reader some hope of Hirshl's liberation by causing him to make repeated visits to the outlying streets of Szybusz where Blume now lives with the family of

Akavia Mazal. This naturally leads the reader to think that perhaps Hirshl will finally seek out Blume and declare his feelings for her. However, Hirshl never actually enters the house in pursuit of his beloved, but he waits outside of it, hoping that Blume will somehow materialize. Night after night Hirshl circles Blume's house like a man performing a religious vigil, waiting for something miraculous to occur. Change, however, is not achieved in Agnon's fictional world through miraculous intervention, but must be initiated through human effort. Similarly, love cannot be brought to fruition without the requisite human effort. In these visits, Hirshl goes so far as to approach Blume's front door, but he stops short of taking any real initiative to confront her. Instead of knocking at her door, he prefers to wait outside in the shadows. Thus, it is not surprising that when Blume does happen to emerge one evening from behind the garden gate, she is so shocked at the sight of Hirshl that she fearfully retreats into the house. Rather than pursuing Blume through the gate, Hirshl stands immobilized outside of it and soon becomes soaked by the rain that starts to fall. He then leans his head against the latch of the gate and begins to weep tears of despair (148 [3:193]).

This small but highly charged incident is pivotal in the novel because it epitomizes, perhaps more than any other event, the anguished longing of the Agnon hero who is filled with passion but is unable to act upon it. It is no wonder then that Agnon chose to use the phrase "upon the latch of the gate" ('*al kapot haman 'ul*)[11] to serve as the title for the entire volume in which *Sipur pashut* appears. The ability to love, for Agnon, is closely related to the ability to conquer fear, doubt, and uncertainty. Without the courage to step over that line, or pass "through the gate" of his own uncertainties, the hero can never achieve the love that he desires. No matter how much longing for love he possesses, the man of inaction will remain forever suspended between his longing and its fulfillment, much like Hirshl who stands weeping in the rain outside of Blume's garden gate.

At the same time, it is legitimate to wonder whether Blume flees from Hirshl because she simply does not care for him anymore. Should the reader regard Hirshl's condition as a mere case of unrequited love? Certainly this would explain Hirshl's lack of aggressiveness in pursuing Blume, for it would be humiliating to impose his affections upon one who is indifferent. However, a careful reading of the novel would suggest otherwise. The novel in fact makes it clear that Blume is still in love with Hirshl, to the extent that she is unable to give her heart to any other. And indeed Blume has many admirers who are vying for her affection, such as the local Zionist activist Getzel Stein and the Socialist leader of Szybusz, Dr. Knabenhut, both of whom she rejects (143, 152-3 [3:188, 197]).[12] Is Blume then secretly hoping and waiting for Hirshl to return to her? If so, why did she flee from him in front of her house?

The narrator gives the reader a clue to this puzzle by telling the reader that although Blume suffered greatly by falling in love with Hirshl and then losing him, she was not ultimately crushed by these experiences. Her reaction in fact to the whole ill-begotten affair is one of stoic acceptance, a response completely opposite to Hirshl's which is marked by restless musing and self-deception. Blume indeed gives the appearance of having emerged relatively unscathed, perhaps due to the fact that she has known suffering and misfortune all her life, and hence possesses the resolute strength of a wounded but tough survivor.[13] In this respect, Blume is very much unlike the typical heroine in the classic romance tale in that she does not wither away or die of lovesickness after losing her beloved,[14] but serenely accepts her lot in life. As the narrator puts it: "anyone talking to her could only have been impressed by the shadow of a smile around her lips that seemed to say: I may have been unlucky, but I managed to land on my feet" (153 [3:197-8]).

It seems likely then that Blume flees from Hirshl outside her door because she is genuinely shocked by his sudden appearance, for unlike Hirshl, she has not been thinking about him obsessively. Blume was not spending her days dreaming about seeing Hirshl again, not only because of the fact that he is married to another woman, but also because seeing him would undoubtedly be a disturbing reminder of a painful past that she has been able to successfully leave behind her, or at least repress.

Of course, Blume's strength and resilience should come as no surprise to the reader, since the novel has consistently portrayed

Szybusz as being composed of strong women and weak men (e.g., Tsirl, Bertha, and Blume versus Boruch Meir, Gedalia, and Hirshl). This "matriarchal" slant provided by the author is certainly anything but an attempt to praise its women, but is rather a lens through which to view its flaws. Agnon might even be suggesting that there is something perverse about a society in which the men are ineffectual and the women are tough-minded, almost as if the camera has got the picture upside down.[15] It is hardly a wonder then that love is strangely absent from Szybusz. Agnon, writing at a time before sexual roles had become blurred, shows that men who are unable to act like men can never achieve love, but are constantly at the mercy of their own inner weakness. Women like Blume fare only slightly better, for if they refuse to settle for a man they can dominate, they will end up alone, albeit stolidly resigned to it. Thus, the reader is told by the narrator that Blume "wanted no more mother's or father's boys, whether they dreamed of Zion or of the millennium" (152 [3:197]). Having lost the man she loved, Blume was happier being alone rather than the wife of a man she would inevitably look down upon.

In contrast to Blume, Hirshl undergoes a distinct psychological change in the novel after that climactic moment when he breaks down weeping upon Blume's gate. Following this incident, he ceases his nightly pilgrimage to Blume's street, a decision which itself seems to initiate a kind of crisis in his life. Up to this point, thinking about Blume had sustained Hirshl, especially in moments of extreme boredom and frustration with his life. Although he had never actually done more than wait longingly outside Blume's door, this at least was something that gave him some hope of change, even if it was a kind of surrogate for real action. But when Blume ran away from him at her door, all of Hirshl's hopes were shattered. Moreover, standing there weeping in the rain, he realized that he had lost his chance with Blume a long time ago, as evidenced by his sudden recollection of the time she had stroked his head in her room and he had fled from her (148 [3:193]).[16] Perceiving this truth, he now had no reason to wander to her house at night, and therefore no purpose left in his life, pitiful as it had been.

Without this nightly activity to sustain him, Hirshl is now left with nothing but his own self to face. And certainly this self is not a pleasant sight to gaze upon. Hence a period of insomnia ensues as Hirshl struggles to avoid facing himself and his own internal weakness. Sleeplessness thus functions as a psychological device, almost resembling an inner force, that is bent on forcing Hirshl to face the person he truly is.[17] Its external manifestation in Hirshl's mind is the rooster that Hirshl blames as the source of his sleeplessness. Every time he feels he is finally falling asleep, he hears the rooster crow and he is woken by it. It even gets to the point where Hirshl fantasizes about killing the rooster so that he may be able to finally sleep (156, 167 [3:201, 211]).

Hirshl's hostility to the rooster is of course a telling indication of his unsureness about his own masculinity,[18] since the word "rooster" in Hebrew (*gever*) is identical to the word for "male." Indeed, the rooster seems to represent all that is instinctively male for Hirshl, i.e., the aggressive urges that Hirshl has repressed most of his life, and which now appear in the guise of the rooster to crow and taunt him. He wishes therefore to rid himself of this incessant reminder of his own failings as a man, and hence his desire to kill the rooster. But Hirshl is unable to do this, because this would mean of course that he would have to escape who he is, for the rooster is actually an undeveloped side of himself. And this is essentially what Hirshl tries to do by "going mad": he tries to escape who he is, at least for a while, in order to avoid looking at himself and his own frustrated masculinity. Consequently, madness is, in this case, the weak man's way of escaping unhappiness, and more importantly of escaping himself, in order to take a rest from his life and the muddle he has made of it.

One of the first signs of Hirshl's impending "madness" occurs in the synagogue when, during morning prayers, he feels tempted to crow like a rooster.[19] He questions in his mind why it is that people think one is crazy if one crows like a rooster, and not crazy if one merely screams like a man (171 [3:215]). Understood symbolically, it seems as if Hirshl perceives that his society condemns the assertion of masculinity as an act of deviance, but accepts other forms of unusual behavior as acceptable. The fact that this realization occurs in a synagogue is also significant, for it is within the traditional religious milieu that Jewish behavioral norms are grounded. One could perhaps argue that the passivity of the Jewish male has its origins in the religious life of the Jews;[20] if so, it would be fitting that it is within this religious setting that Hirshl experiences the temptation to release his male aggression, but then quickly stifles it in fear of being condemned. It is only later when he is alone in the forest that he feels free from societal condemnation to express himself as he wills.

If one looks closely at Hirshl's words during the height of his "madness" scene in the forest, one notices that the rooster continues to play a major role in his consciousness. Hirshl clearly identifies with the rooster but fights to deny it, being obviously terrified of the likeness. To those who find him in the forest he screams, "Don't cut my throat! I'm not a rooster! I'm not!" (174 [3:218]). Insisting again and again that he is not a rooster, he instead claims affinity with a frog that goes "ga ga ga."[21]

The symbolic significance of the frog is twofold, for not only is a frog or toad synonymous with groveling and obsequiousness (i.e., as in being a "toady"), but it also has a rich history in terms of the fairy tale. Princes and those of noble birth are often turned into frogs by wizards or other evildoers, and are only redeemed from this humiliating state by the love of a fair maiden.[22] Accordingly, it could be argued that the mythic structure of this novel is no less than the story of Hirshl himself as a kind of frog-prince, a youth of promise who has been turned into a lowly creature by his mother and the matriarchal society she represents; as a "frog," his only hope of regaining his manhood (both literally and figuratively) is by means of the love of the fair maiden Blume Nacht. But in the fairy tale, the love of the maiden must be *earned,* which is no simple task, since as a frog there is little likelihood of acquiring the maiden's affections. It requires sheer persistence and strength of deed and mind.[23] Of course, this is where Hirshl fails, and the story becomes stuck at this very juncture. This is because without some dynamic initiative on Hirshl's part, he will not only never win the maiden, but he will also be doomed to remain a frog (i.e., a lowly, miserable creature) for the rest of his days.[24]

Despite Hirshl's abnormal behavior in the forest, however, it must be recognized that he is actually in full control of his actions. This is why the word "madness" should be used with inverted commas when referring to Hirshl, for the narrator makes it sufficiently clear in the novel that Hirshl is in fact quite sane.[25] Note how explicitly this is disclosed:

> As bizarrely as he was acting, Hirshl had his wits about him. He knew that, unlike his mother's grandfather who wore a chamber pot on his head, he could not make a hat of a shoe, and that, unlike his maternal uncle who ran off to the forest for good, he would have to go home in the end. (173 [3:216-17])

It is not too difficult to conclude, then, that Hirshl is feigning madness. But if this is so, why would he choose to do this, and for what purpose?

Hirshl's "madness" should actually come as no surprise to the reader because, in a sense, it is a culmination of what has been revealed already about Hirshl up to this point. All along, Hirshl's way of responding to the unhappy circumstances of his life has been to internalize his own dissent. His "mad" episode in the forest merely takes this one step further, in that Hirshl briefly allows his inner thoughts to be expressed aloud. This is, in effect, a cry for help and can be seen as Hirshl's last-ditch effort to be saved from the misery of his life with Mina.[26] But it is a weak man's way of trying to effect change. Hirshl obviously prefers to feign madness and suffer the shame of being regarded as a lunatic, rather than change the course of his life by direct means.and risk what he views as a worse form of censure by his family and community.[27] Going "mad" wins Hirshl a respite, albeit temporary, from his life as he knew it. Seen more cynically, it gives Hirshl a pleasant holiday from a wife he despises, and also from the type of disaffected husband he himself has become.

The type of treatment Hirshl receives at the sanatorium to which he is sent lends further support to the contention that Hirshl suffers less from "madness" than from an acute case of internal frustration coupled with cowardice, being trapped as he is in a loathsome marriage that he is afraid to dissolve. Hirshl's soundness of mind is proven by the mere fact alone that he recovers his mental balance shortly after his arrival at the sanatorium despite the astonishing fact that the neurologist, Dr. Langsam, barely submits Hirshl to any medicinal or psychoanalytic treatments. In point of fact, the elderly Dr. Langsam takes little interest in Hirshl's psychological problems, and instead he spends their sessions together regaling Hirshl with sentimental stories about his *own* past. This is undoubtedly Agnon's subtle way of poking fun at the mystique surrounding the psychoanalyst, whom he portrays here as being no different than a simple storyteller.[28] And indeed Dr. Langsam suffers from his own problems: his wife, the reader soon learns, had committed suicide after an unhappy love affair with another man (191 [3:234]). It is no wonder then that Dr. Langsam is in no position to properly heal others, for his own life is in disarray—a situation surely deserving the old adage, "Physician, heal thyself!"[29]

Hirshl's "recovery" therefore seems to have less to do with what Dr. Langsam does for him as a therapist, than it does with what the doctor incidentally achieves through the telling of his nostalgic tales about the past. Evoking the *shtetl* of his childhood to Hirshl, Dr. Langsam depicts the meek and downtrodden Jews of his past as those who possess intrinsic beauty, goodness, and wisdom. In particular, he is fond of telling Hirshl about the blind beggars who used to sing their sad songs in the marketplace of his town. Sometimes the doctor would even sing some of these haunting tunes to Hirshl during their sessions, charming him with their sad melodies.[30]

Although Dr. Langsam's songs and stories seem to lull Hirshl into a state of relative calm, one should recognize that they are probably the last thing Hirshl truly needs. The doctor's romantic view of the Jew as meek and long suffering is certainly no help to Hirshl, who is plagued by the same personality traits the doctor idealizes. Indeed, these are the very traits that Dr. Langsam found so appealing in Hirshl when he first arrived at the sanatorium. Note how the narrator describes the doctor's initial response to Hirshl: "[t]he combination of meekness, resignation, and sadness that he saw in Hirshl's face made the old doctor take an instant liking to him" (178 [3:222]). This reveals precisely why Hirshl cannot possibly be cured by the likes of Dr. Langsam, for the doctor's view of Hirshl is all askew.[31] Any perceptive reader can see that Hirshl's unhappiness stems from the fact that he is too meek to act upon his desires, whereas the doctor regards this same meekness as Hirshl's virtue. That is why Dr. Langsam's "treatment" serves only to perpetuate Hirshl's problems, for the doctor romanticizes and celebrates such meekness rather than seeing it as a liability.

Consequently, Hirshl's "recovery" at the sanatorium is illusory and ultimately short lived. As soon as Hirshl receives a telegram that Mina has given birth to a son, his old symptoms of insomnia and obsessiveness return all the more powerfully. His sessions with the doctor had merely provided him with a temporary holiday from his wife; as soon as he is forced to think of her again, his pain and suffering return with a vengeance.

Hirshl experiences a vivid nightmare[32] during this period of anguished sleeplessness in the sanatorium, a nightmare which seems to convey to the reader the truth about Hirshl's psychological state (193 [3:236]). Through a series of symbols, Hirshl's nightmare discloses the tragic facts of his life which he is unable to face during waking hours, but which nonetheless emerge through his unconscious in the form of a dream.[33] The setting of the nightmare is Szybusz, but it is so shrunken in size that it fits into the palm of Hirshl's hand, an image likely representing Hirshl's unconscious view of his town as stunted, shrunken, and deformed.[34] Held between Hirshl's fingers is a blind beggar similar to those romantically described by Dr. Langsam, except that in Hirshl's dream the beggar is not singing beautiful sad tunes, but a bizarre song about "the snow that fell on the ground where the froggies grazed" (193 [3:236]). The reader will of course recall that this is the same song about frogs that Hirshl sang during his "mad" episode in the forest. In fact, it is here in the dream that the distinction between Hirshl and the blind beggar becomes blurred so that they begin to merge into one character. In other words, the reader begins to recognize that Hirshl sees *himself* as a kind of "blind beggar"—"blind" in that he is unable to see the tragic truth about his life, and a "beggar" in that he is profoundly needy, albeit not materially but emotionally. It is also significant that the song that the blind beggar sings in the nightmare seems in Hirshl's mind to go on forever, perhaps indicating that Hirshl's habit of "closing his eyes" to his emotional needs has become a pattern that repeats itself without end.[35]

The sudden appearance in the dream of a cloaked woman who bends down and offers Hirshl cake is clearly a symbolic reference to Blume Nacht, who had indeed brought cake with her to the Hurvitz home on her arrival there. It is important to recall that at the beginning of the novel it was due to Blume's cake that Hirshl first asserted himself against his mother, taking Blume's side against the domineering influence of Tsirl.[36] Here in the dream, however, Hirshl is unable to take the cake from the cloaked woman because just as he is about to reach for it, a man suddenly appears and throws coins into Hirshl's eyes, coins which grow upon his eyes into two mountains and blind his vision.[37]

As for the cake, being an object that is both special and sweet, it clearly symbolizes Blume's love for Hirshl that was offered to him but was not accepted by him. The dream reveals that Hirshl knows in his subconscious that Blume had indeed been in love with him, and that it was his own failure to receive that love which resulted in his loss of her. This, of course, is contrary to his stubborn insistence during his waking hours that it was Blume who had rejected *him*.

It is not difficult to interpret the significance of the coins in the dream, for the novel has already made it clear that "throwing [and "piling up"] coins," i.e., making money, is the ruling passion of Hirshl's parents, and indeed of Szybusz society as a whole.[38] The fact that coins are the objects that blind Hirshl in the dream, preventing him from accepting the cake, is undoubtedly a symbolic way of saying that it was money that had been the true obstacle blinding Hirshl and causing him to reject Blume's love. It is no wonder, then, that Hirshl is unable to admit this to himself during his waking hours, for it is a hard and bitter truth to face that he had chosen money and material ease over the true love of a woman.

Moreover, it is certainly not accidental that the coins thrown at Hirshl should remind the reader once again of Hirshl being a kind of "beggar," for who else do people throw coins at if not at beggars. Also, the fact that the coins land on Hirshl's eyes and prevent him from seeing, reinforces the notion that Hirshl is "blind." If one had previously been in doubt about whether Hirshl's apparent identification with the blind beggar is authentic, it is surely validated again by these symbolic events in his dream.

Furthermore, the fact that the coins upon Hirshl's eyes grow into two mountains could be seen as a symbolic reference to the piles of coins that Tsirl and Boruch Meir took such delight in counting earlier in the novel.[39] Therefore, it is not just any coins that prevent Hirshl from accepting Blume's love, but it is the money accumulated so greedily by his parents that is the greatest obstacle preventing his union with Blume. Also, mountains are huge obstructions that are difficult to surmount, thereby reinforcing Hirshl's painful awareness that his parents' money is a mountainous barrier keeping him permanently separated from the woman he loves.

The dream ends with Hirshl screaming and sobbing but no one hears him because his voice is drowned out by the sound of carriage wheels. Hirshl's cry of anguish in the dream to which no one responds is not only a painful revelation of how strongly he feels that his needs and wants have been ignored by those around him, but may also be a symbolic reference to Hirshl's bout of "insanity" in the forest, where he shouted and babbled to the point of incoherence. The dream seems to be telling him that even that desperate episode in the forest will never be "heard" by the people of Szybusz, i.e., they will never understand what drove him to "insanity." In other words, Hirshl's dream attempts to make him face the fact that even his last desperate cry for help through a form of "madness" has fallen on deaf ears.

It is significant that the noise of carriage wheels in the dream that drowns out Hirshl's crying and sobbing is reminiscent of an earlier scene in the novel that may provide a vital clue toward understanding its full meaning. This is because the reader has already heard about "carriage wheels" in relation to another dream in the novel—Blume's dream on the first night she slept at the Hurvitz home (4-5 [3:56]). In that dream, Blume is sitting in a wagon and when she disembarks, the horses bolt and begin to run wild, dragging the wagon wildly through the streets. She covers her eyes to avoid seeing the catastrophe she fears will result. Here, the image of the wagon running wild seems to function as a kind of premonition of the danger Blume subconsciously fears is awaiting her in this new place to which she has indeed just arrived by wagon.[40] When she awakens from the dream, the first sound she hears is the noise of carriage wheels outside her window, and in fact that sound is one of the first impressions of Szybusz that she has.

Compounded with the wild image of the wagon in her dream, the noise of carriage wheels now sounds an ominous note that not only represents the clang and clamor of merchant life, but also the threat that everything bound up with this life may pose a danger for her in the future.

It follows then that Hirshl's dream at the sanatorium toward the end of the novel can be seen as a kind of completion of Blume's dream at the beginning of the story. The noise of carriage wheels is similarly malevolent in Hirshl's dream, for their sound prevents his cry of anguish from being heard. It is as if the same clamorous sounds of merchant life that Blume sensed would lead to misery, have managed to also muzzle Hirshl's unhappiness about the course of his own life. In fact, Hirshl's dream tells the reader what eventually happened to the runaway carriage that Blume originally dreamt about on her first night in Szybusz: the carriage, symbolizing the destructive influence of money within the town, is shown to be charging through Hirshl's life and seizing control of his fate. That is, the dictates of money that govern Szybusz ensure that the prevailing status quo is upheld. In Hirshl's case, this means that a prosperous merchant's son cannot possibly marry a penniless orphan, no matter how much he loves her. His dream shows that even when he tried in his own distorted way to rebel against this fact (i.e., to go "mad"), his cries of protest fell on deaf ears. And perhaps this is the way it shall remain for Hirshl. Like a portent of the future, the dream reveals that even Hirshl's "madness" will never nullify his union with Mina, for at the end of the dream it is not Blume who he sees, but another woman who takes her place, bearing a strange resemblance to none other than his wife Mina.

Indeed, it may come as a surprise to the reader that when Hirshl is finally able to uncover his eyes in his dream, what he sees is no longer a "Blume-like" character serving him a piece of cake as at the beginning of the dream. Instead, he sees the "slender and attractive" Sophia Gildenhorn who bears "a friendly smile" and smells "of something good," riding in the very carriage that had been noisily drowning out his cries. But why Sophia Gildenhorn and not Mina herself? This is likely because Sophia is precisely the type of frivolous woman who is most valued in Szybusz, and is the ideal to which Mina aspires—a woman whose life revolves around parties, gossip, sweet-smelling cologne, and being at the center of her social set. Hirshl despises this sort of woman but, as we know, is burdened with one nonetheless, for his wife Mina is merely a less glamorous imitation of the Sophia Gildenhorn "type."

Consequently, the dream leaves the reader with the distinct sense that despite all the rest and "therapy" Hirshl received at the sanatorium, he has not surrendered his most dearly held hopes and passions. Underneath he is still a man deeply dissatisfied with the compromises he has made in his life, and painfully cognizant of the weakness of his own nature which allowed such compromises to be made. It is no wonder, then, that immediately following this dream Hirshl again becomes a "nervous wreck" (193 [3:236]), so much so that the narrator tells us that "a great sorrow haunted his dazed eyes, which ached with an inner feeling of devastation" (193 [3:237]). The dream indeed suggests that Hirshl subconsciously knows that his bout of "madness" has failed to loosen Mina's hold on him, for just as she sits waiting for him at the end of the dream in the guise of Sophia Gildenhorn, so Mina in reality is waiting for him at home unchanged and unlikely to ever change.

It makes sense, then, that Hirshl soon tires of playing the role of the lunatic, perhaps because he has become painfully aware of its uselessness as a ploy to effect change in his.life. Now, looking around him in the sanatorium, he sees people who are *truly* mad and, sharing no true affinity with them, he begins to panic that perhaps he will never be released. Hirshl even begins to fear that he may die there at the sanatorium, and feeling "so close to the reality of death" (195 [3:239]), he knows he must get out. It is as if Hirshl suddenly awakens to the fact that his attempt at "madness" might have gotten him into a worse predicament than he anticipated. Therefore, it is not accidental that upon realizing that he could be locked up as a lunatic forever, Hirshl begins to think about his old life in Szybusz again. In fact, faced with the likelihood of ending his days confined to a sanatorium, even the thought of returning to Szybusz starts to look good to him. As a result, Hirshl decides that he is "back to normal" (195 [3:239]), and his behavior in the sanatorium becomes so exemplary that before long Dr. Langsam is compelled to send him home.

Upon his return, Hirshl is described as being fit, bearded, and tanned (201 [3:244])—in fact, more like someone who had been holidaying at a resort than one confined to a mental institution. It should be recalled that Hirshl's stay at the sanatorium had many of the characteristics of a relaxing vacation; he has spent much of his time there playing games of chess and gardening, while being pampered with daily rubdowns, glasses of wine, and "entertainment" provided by the doctor's personal stories and songs (189 [3:232]).[41] Agnon seems to be showing that just as Hirshl's "madness" was a sham, so is the "cure" that patients like Hirshl receive in such institutions. In other words, Agnon is poking fun at the pretensions of such places that claim to offer professional psychological treatment, when all they do in reality is function as a kind of vacation resort for the world-weary.

Hirshl in fact has not been "cured," for despite his return to home and hearth he still fails to reconcile himself to his marriage to Mina. A careful reading of the last six chapters of the novel reveals that Hirshl remains permanently dissatisfied with his marriage, and continues to dwell on Blume Nacht right up until the very end of the story. Indeed, this is made perfectly clear in the novel even during Hirshl's first weeks home:

> But what happiness could there be without love, and what child would want a childhood in which his parents did not love each other? Hirshl wondered whether it was possible for a Jew to hate his wife—and yet, though he did not really hate Mina, not loving her was almost as bad. Had his heart not been another's he might have been happy with the woman he had. More than one man who failed to marry the wife of his choice had shared a contented life with someone else in the end. But Hirshl had given his heart away and no longer had it to share. (204 [3:246-7])

Despite the seeming finality of this statement, Hirshl is shown to subsequently undergo a change of attitude toward his wife in the last two chapters of the novel. Agnon in fact contrives the plot in such a way as to make it seem as if Hirshl experiences a permanent change in his feelings toward Mina, to the surprising extent that suddenly their relationship seems to be miraculously blossoming into—of all unlikely things—love! But this entire turn of events should be read with caution, for there are a number of telling incidents in these last two chapters that reveal a different story. I would in fact contend that Hirshl never actually goes through any kind of true change of heart or catharsis in the novel, despite Agnon's playful attempt to make it *appear* as if he has.

But why would Agnon try to convince the reader that Hirshl has suddenly found true love with the wife he had previously found intolerable, and then subsequently turn the tables on the reader as if it was only a playful ruse on Agnon's part? Before attempting to answer this question, it is essential to first look closely at the particular events surrounding those two key final chapters. This should convince the careful reader that, despite appearances to the contrary, Hirshl's change of heart toward his wife is not only dubious but based on distorted premises.

The main event that stimulates "love" between Hirshl and Mina is, oddly enough, the decision to send away their first and only child Meshulam to live with Mina's parents in the countryside. The ostensible reason for doing so is because of Meshulam's poor health, the argument being that if he were sent out of the city he would begin to physically thrive. It is at this point in the novel that Hirshl and Mina begin a kind of "second honeymoon." The message here seems to be clear: now that their child is gone, they can finally discover true love together. However, anyone who thinks about this for more than a moment should agree that this is a strange and even *perverse* precondition for love to occur between man and wife. The fact that they needed to rid themselves of their son in order to love each other, almost like a sacrifice to a jealous god, is not only disturbing but goes against all natural instincts of parental love and loyalty.[42] Even if one were to argue that perhaps they needed the time alone together in order to kindle their romance, the fact that they never attempt to bring Meshulam home again is a sign that there is something terribly amiss in their newfound "Paradise" (223 [3:266]).

The second event that causes the reader to doubt the seriousness of Hirshl's and Mina's transformed relationship occurs during their trip to the country to visit Meshulam. While walking in the snow, Hirshl and Mina come upon a blind beggar singing songs reminiscent of those described by Dr. Langsam at the sanatorium.

The sight of the beggar causes Hirshl to react with sudden violence: he grabs Mina's arm with force and speaks so harshly to her that it "sent a shiver down her spine" (226 [3:268]). But Hirshl's explosive response should not surprise the reader, for we have already witnessed how deeply Hirshl identifies the blind beggar with himself. Indeed, as evidenced by his dream at the sanatorium, Hirshl subconsciously regards the figure of the blind beggar as a symbolic representative of the truth about his inner self—i.e., about his profound emotional needs to which he has been "blind."[43] Seeing such a figure clearly arouses terror in Hirshl because he has obviously not faced this truth about himself in his conscious life, but has merely denied its existence. This incident confirms our suspicions: Hirshl's "cure" at the sanatorium and his subsequent "transformation" into a loving husband are merely part of a thin veneer covering up a mind that is just as confused and unsteady as it was before. And certainly it does not take long for this veneer to crack: the mere sight of the blind beggar pierces Hirshl's facade and seems to force him to recall that he is still the same unhappy person he had been striving to forget.

After this incident, it is no wonder that, as the reader is told, Hirshl has again become "restless" (226 [3:268]), shifting from extreme happiness to extreme sadness. But this restlessness also does not last for long, for Hirshl soon "settled down" (226 [3:268]). The reader, however, is left with a lingering uncertainty about how "settled" and content Hirshl truly is,[44] since the chapter ends on a faint but telling discordant note that presents a different story. The reader is told that Hirshl is relieved that he and Mina do not have a piano, since it "spared him" from having to listen to Mina play it (226 [3:268]). Although this remark *seems* inconsequential, it is surely significant that it ends a chapter, thereby leaving the reader with the distinct sense that Hirshl still finds life with Mina barely tolerable. But the difference now from earlier in the novel is that Hirshl has given up trying to change his plight and instead has learned to conform to it. Like other members of Szybusz society, Hirshl now does what is expected of him, even if this means pretending to be in love with a wife whose mere presence he can hardly bear.

But why would Agnon play with the reader, making it *appear* as if Hirshl has somehow attained a state of wedded bliss at the end of the novel? Why does Agnon only reveal the truth of Hirshl's situation through subtle hints and faintly discordant notes? This is a technique that I believe Agnon uses purposefully in order to challenge the intelligent reader, on the assumption that truth is not found on the surface of things, but is hidden in its subtleties.[45] Thus, in portraying *Hirshl's* self-deception, Agnon tries to also deceive the *reader* into believing Hirshl's claims. Agnon's challenge thus becomes as follows: will we, as readers, be canny enough to see that Hirshl is deceiving himself about his own happiness at the end of the novel? Or will we ourselves become, as it were, mere versions of Hirshl Hurvitz, closing our eyes to the contradictions, and reading the story as if it utters a simple hopeful message at the end?

I would contend that the astute reader will *not* find a hopeful message at the close of the novel,[46] especially if he looks closely at Hirshl's final conversation with Mina regarding whether they can love more than one child. It should be recalled that Hirshl and Mina are now parents of a second son, and are apparently in a state of delirious happiness about his birth. But the issue now at stake is what to do about their first son Meshulam, who had been sent to live with Mina's parents, and as yet has not been brought back to live with his own parents. Although Hirshl and Mina agree in this conversation that Meshulam is better off with Mina's parents, Hirshl's reasoning behind this decision discloses an odd logic on his part. He says, "love can't be divided. . . . Love comes [to us][47] only when no one stands between it and us" (229 [3:271-2]).

At first glance, this statement could seem to be merely Hirshl's way of reflecting on his own experience of discovering love with his wife after finally abandoning his thoughts of Blume. And certainly Agnon seems to encourage such a reading, since he follows Hirshl's statement with the ironic quip, "God in heaven knew that he [Hirshl] was thinking only of the baby" (229 [3:272]). In other words, this line seems to imply that Hirshl was tacitly referring to Blume Nacht, who had once stood in the way of Hirshl's and Mina's love for each other, but who is now no longer in Hirshl's thoughts and hence is not an obstacle to his love for Mina.[48]

It is my view, however, that giving such an interpretation to the end of the novel would be to entirely miss the point of Agnon's irony.[49] Even if Hirshl *is* philosophizing about the nature of love based on his painful experience with Blume Nacht, the fact that he extends the same logic to his own son (i.e., needing to renounce one child for the sake of the other) makes no sense whatsoever. Moreover, the narrator lets the reader know that it is not as if Meshulam is so well treated by Mina's parents. We are told that they are "no longer young and have forgotten how to talk to a child," and that Meshulam's new brother "had it better" than him (229 [3:271]). Therefore, it must be asked, what sort of "happiness" could Hirshl and Mina have discovered if it is based on the abandonment of their own child?[50] In fact, if this truly is Hirshl's logic, then I believe it would be reasonable to conclude that he has gained no understanding of the nature of love from his past experiences, and that he is incapable of loving anyone, including his wife and children.

Alternatively, the end of the novel can be read in a wholly different light, one that I think is more faithful to the entire unfolding of Hirshl's psychological profile. This reading interprets Hirshl's final remark that "love can't be divided" to be an indication of his devoted attachment to Blume Nacht which still keeps him from ever being able to truly give his heart to his wife. That would explain why he has such a perverse attitude toward his own children, for they are the fruit of Mina's womb, rather than Blume's. The end, therefore, should be read in light of the novel as a whole.[51] Hirshl is still the same lovelorn character whose mind is distorted by having been coerced into marrying the wrong woman. Consequently, his unnatural attitude toward his own child at the end of the novel shows that this is what happens to a man in a society where the natural path of love is blocked. The story of Hirshl and Blume should have been a simple one, resulting in a happy marriage and the promise of children beloved by their parents; instead, because of the strange vicissitudes of Jewish life, Agnon shows us a marriage of convenience that becomes tolerable only due to sheer lack of an alternative, with the fruit of such a union resulting in a child who is ultimately unloved and unwanted. Surely this is the final tragic note of the novel that decisively undercuts any pretense of a "happy ending"—the abandoned child of Hirshl and Mina who remains the unhappy product of a misguided and loveless match.

Notes

1. Note also that the narrator here compares the candles under the wedding canopy to "bitterly crying eyes" (105 [3:151]), obviously suggesting an underlying unhappiness despite the supposed joyousness of the occasion. For an incisive discussion of the "candle" motif in *Sipur pashut*, see Dov Landau, *Misignon le-mashma'ut be-sipure Shai 'Agnon* (Tel Aviv, Israel: Eked, 1988), 105-9.

2. In this split between Hirshl's thoughts and actions, Baruch Hochman detects a similarity to the character of Emma Bovary in Flaubert's *Madame Bovary*. See Baruch Hochman, *The Fiction of S. Y. Agnon* (Ithaca, N. Y.: Cornell University Press, 1970), 95-6. Robert Alter also discusses the general influence of Flaubert's literary technique on Agnon. Cf. Robert Alter, *Hebrew and Modernity* (Bloomington: University of Indiana, 1994), 134-53. The influence of Flaubert on Agnon seems likely, since in a letter written in 1916 by Agnon to his friend and patron Zalman Schocken, he singles out Flaubert for praise. See *Sh. Y. Agnon—Sh. Z. Shoken: hilufe igrot* (Jerusalem: Schocken, 1991), 36-8.

3. This notion will be discussed further in my next chapter on the significance of Jewish history and its bearing on love in the novel.

4. The narrator tells us that Hirshl made a conscious decision to banish certain thoughts from his mind. The narrator states, "Hirshl had not thought of Akavia Mazal for a long time. Once he had mused often about this man who had fallen in love with his ex-pupil's daughter Tirza, who sat talking with her friend Blume about her husband and young Hirshl Hurvitz. One day, however, Hirshl had sat down with himself and decided to put such thoughts out of his mind" (114 [3:160]). It does not take too much imagination to calculate *when* Hirshl banished such thoughts—after his marriage to Mina.

5. In his book on Agnon, Amos Oz makes much of the sexual relationship between Hirshl and Mina, claiming that by the end of the novel Hirshl realizes that it is Mina who is his true beloved. Moreover, Oz argues that in contrast to Mina's innate eroticism, Blume Nacht is frigid, and is never able to give Hirshl the love that he so desperately needs. See Amos Oz, *Shtikat Ha-shamayim: Agnon Mishtomem 'Al Elohim* (Jerusalem: Keter, 1993), 39-72. Although Oz's interpretation is novel, I do not think that it adequately takes into account all the relevant details of the text. First, it ignores Agnon's clearly placed erotic hints about Blume. For example, in the scene where Blume reenters her bedroom while Hirshl lies on her bed, she makes the bold move of stroking Hirshl's head. It should be noted that in this social milieu, not only would it be improper for a young unmarried couple to be alone together in a girl's bedroom, but the idea of a girl initiating physical contact likely would be viewed as shocking if not sexually immoral. Consider also that it is then *Hirshl* who gets up and flees the room, not Blume (34 [3:82-3]). This is not even to mention the many passages in the novel where Hirshl expresses his abhorrence for Mina, which Oz does not take seriously and is able to "explain away" by means of a psychoanalytic, rather than a truly literary, approach to the text. For a thorough

critique of Oz's view of Blume Nacht, see Nitza Ben-Dov, *Ahavot lo me'usharot* (Leiden, The Netherlands: E. J. Brill, 1993), 270-93.

6. For example, Hirshl enjoys his newfound status as a householder, and it is upon his suggestion that he and Mina begin to invite their parents to dine with them on a regular basis (119 [3:165]). Similarly, Hirshl is glad to find himself thrust into the center of the Szybusz social set by opening his home in the evenings to the Gildenhorns and their crowd of freeloaders and jokers (123 [3:169]). But all of this is short-lived, for Hirshl begins to tire of the social whirl once the initial excitement of it wears off.

7. Note how Hirshl recoils when Mina snuggles close to him, and in his mind he compares her to a coat that one is forced to wear all the time but that "never keeps you warm" (123 [3:169]).

8. Malka Shaked points out that Hirshl switches from third person to first person in the middle of telling Mina about his mad uncle (e.g., switching from "libo" to "libi"), an indication that Hirshl is really speaking about himself when relaying the story of his uncle's unhappy fate. See Malka Shaked, "Ha-im haya Hirshl meshug'a? Likrat ra'ya pluralistit shel ha-'alilah be-*Sipur pashut*," *Hasifrut* 32 (June 1982): 132-47.

9. Baruch Kurzweil makes the point that Hirshl creates an imaginary home ("bayit medumeh") within his own mind in order to effect a kind of escape from his intolerable life with his parents and then later with Mina. See Baruch Kurzweil, *Masot 'al sipure Shai 'Agnon* (Tel Aviv, Israel: Schocken, 1970), 216.

10. Although some feminist critics strive to prove that this is not the ruling pattern (or, if it is, then it must be the result of a patriarchal conspiracy!), I would argue that the hero in literature is by necessity the initiator of action rather than the passive receptor. In recent years, several feminists have attempted to dislodge the notion of the male hero and rewrite the fairy tale. There is little evidence, however, that these new "fairy tales" have unseated the old. Cf. Jack D. Zipes, ed., *Don't Bet on the Prince: Contemporary Feminist Fairy Tales in North America and England* (New York: Methuen, 1986); and Madonna Kolbenschlag, *Kiss Sleeping Beauty Goodbye* (Garden City, N. Y.: Doubleday, 1979).

11. Note that this phrase is usually translated as "on the handles of the lock," but since I am using Halkin's English translation of the novel as the source of quotations for this work, I am using his phraseology for consistency in my work. Of course, the origin of the phrase is the Song of Songs 5:5. Certainly Agnon's use of this phrase at this pivotal point in the novel has some similarity to the context of the biblical text, in which the object of desire is also unattainable. At the same time, there is something ironic about the comparison as well, for how *unlike* a biblical hero is Hirshl Hurvitz, a young man who has no capacity to articulate his desires, not to mention the capacity to act on them!

12. For example, when Getzel Stein pursues Blume, the reader is told that she "drove him away." The narrator then asks rhetorically, "Could it be that her heart was still pledged to Hirshl, even though he was married and no longer free?" (143 [3:188-9]).

13. Cf. Amos Oz, who cites Blume's past sufferings to explain her "coldness." Oz, *Shtikat Hashamayim,* 39-72.

14. For a discussion of this phenomenon in both its medieval and modern forms, see chapters 4 and 13 in Irving Singer, *The Nature of Love,* vol. 2 (Chicago: University of Chicago Press, 1984), 88-126; 432-81.

15. See my earlier discussion of the topsy-turvy nature of Szybusz in chapter 2 above. Also, see my previous discussion of Hirshl's inverted notions about women and courtship in chapter 3 above.

16. Note that in Hebrew the word Agnon uses in this context to describe the image of Blume that appears before Hirshl is "ikoni" (i.e., "icon"), perhaps signifying an almost *religious* devotion to her.

17. Kurzweil interprets Hirshl's insomnia as an unconscious means of escaping his marital bed with Mina, whom he despises. Kurzweil also points out that Hirshl is unable to admit to himself that he would like to kill his wife, and therefore redirects this latent hostility to his wife toward the rooster who ostensibly keeps him from being able to sleep. In Kurzweil's reading, the hated rooster is a symbolic representation of Mina, who has "wasted" Hirshl's male potency. See Kurzweil, *Masot 'al sipure Shai 'Agnon,* 220.

18. There have been many discussions of the "rooster" motif and its relationship to Hirshl's lack of masculinity, the first of such being initiated by Kurzweil, *Masot 'al sipure Shai 'Agnon,* 216-23. A new twist has been added to this by David Aberbach, who has made a case for interpreting Hirshl's obsession with the rooster as relating to what Aberbach sees as Hirshl's latent homosexuality. To support his argument, Aberbach uses the scenes in which Hirshl desires to kiss the soft hands of Yona Toyber. Although Aberbach builds a fairly strong case for this line of interpretation, I think that he takes it much too far in that direction. To my mind, the main theme of the novel is Hirshl's unconsummated desire for Blume Nacht, with the plot outlining how the forces both *within* him and *around* him prevent that union from ever coming to fruition. Although one of those forces preventing this union is undoubtedly Hirshl's confusion about his male identity (as certainly evidenced by the scenes with Toyber), I do not think there is sufficient evidence within the text to support a reading of latent homosexuality as a key to Hirshl's psychology. See David Aberbach, "Fantasies of Deviance in Mendele and Agnon," *AJS Review* 19, no. 1 (1994): 45-60.

19. Note the similarity here to the Hasidic folk tale about the prince who thought he was a rooster. In that tale the prince, like Hirshl, is also an only child. And also like Hirshl, he is expected by his parents to follow in their footsteps, and in the case of the prince become a grand ruler like themselves. However, after commanding his father's army and winning many battles, the prince returns home and begins to behave like a rooster. He is then "cured" by an old man who, like Dr. Langsam, utilizes no traditional remedies, but instead talks to him for seven days. The story ends by saying that, although the prince was cured and he "resumed his princely role . . . in his heart of hearts, however, he still thought himself a rooster pretending to be a human being." See Tzvi Rabinowicz, ed., *The Prince Who Turned Into a Rooster* (Northvale, N.J.: Jason Aronson, 1993), 253-55.

20. Albert Memmi expresses a similar idea in his work *The Liberation of the Jew* (New York: Viking, 1973), 297-8. I delve further into the question of the relationship between love and religion in chapter 5 below.

21. Dina Stern identifies these as the sounds a baby makes, and interprets them in psychoanalytic terms as an attempt by Hirshl to return to the womb, i.e., not grow up. See Dina Stern, "Ba'ayot ha-talut ve-hizdahut be-haye Hirshl Hurvitz: 'iyyun sifruti-psychologi be-*Sipur pashut* le-Shai 'Agnon," *Bi-Sadeh Hemed* 13 (1971): 296-303. In contrast, Lev Hakak argues that the frog sounds ("ga-ga-ga") represent Hirshl's longing for Blume, deriving this interpretation from the Hebrew word for yearning "ga'agu'im". See Lev Hakak, "Motif ha-tarnigol be-*Sipur pashut* le-Shai 'Agnon," *Hasifrut* 4, no. 4 (1973): 713-25. I think this interpretation is somewhat overstated, since there are many other words in Hebrew that begin with the syllable "ga." I believe the tale of the frog-prince is a more plausible source, especially since the story of Hirshl's love for Blume is structurally similar to that of the classic love story and fairy tale. (See chapter 1 above, as well as chapter 4, note 23 below.)

22. See Iona and Peter Opie, *The Classic Fairy Tale* (London: Oxford University Press, 1974), 183-6.

23. Note that in the frog-prince tale, the frog is finally able to reverse the spell upon him and turn back into a prince by means of his final deed—lying down on the bed of the maiden (Opie, *The Classic Fairy Tale,* 183-6). It is perhaps not coincidental that in *Sipur pashut*, Hirshl too lies down on Blume's bed. However, unlike the mythical frog, Hirshl does not remain there, but instead runs away in panic after Blume strokes his head. Perhaps if he had remained there, his story might have also had a happy ending, like that of the mythical frog-prince!

24. Dov Landau makes a similar point in his discussion of irony in Agnon. He points to the fact that during Hirshl's insomnia, he thinks about two biblical characters, Jacob and Elkanah, both of whom were forced to marry women they did not love, but who remained determined to finally marry women they did love (i.e., Rachel and Hannah). These biblical heroes finally succeeded in winning their beloved ones by means of their own strength of will. But as Landau points out, this is an ironic comparison because, although Hirshl may have had latent aspirations to be like these biblical figures, the truth is that he possessed none of their heroic qualities. See Dov Landau, *Mi-signon le-mashma'ut be-sipure Shai 'Agnon*, 154-5.

25. In a detailed discussion of the question of Hirshl's madness, Malka Shaked also considers whether his madness is feigned. In fact, she outlines four separate possible interpretations of this problem: 1. Hirshl indeed went mad, due to the lack of love in his life; 2. Hirshl truly went mad, due to hereditary mental illness; 3. Hirshl feigned madness as a rebellion against his unhappy marriage and his domineering mother who coerced him into it; 4. Hirshl feigned madness in order to escape the draft. In the end, she comes to the conclusion that all four interpretations are equally plausible, and that the ironic ambiguities within the text itself encourage the reader to consider all of the interpretations listed above. See Malka Shaked, "Ha-im haya Hirshl meshug'a?, 132-47. With all due respect to the thoroughness of Ms. Shaked's article, I differ from her

entirely in respect to the *premise* of her stance. I think that it is requisite for the understanding of literature to make distinctions between those interpretations that are *more* convincing versus those that are *less* so. The unwillingness to make such distinctions leads to a kind of literary relativism, in which all readings become equally plausible, to the point that the text gets lost under the weight of possible readings. Stanley Fish to the contrary, I believe there *is* a text in this class! For a thorough discussion of this subject, see E. D. Hirsch, Jr., *Validity in Interpretation* (New Haven, Conn.: Yale University Press, 1967).

26. Note that not long before Hirshl's outbreak of "madness" on that fateful day in the forest, he seems to have hit bottom in terms of his relationship with Mina, and he actually expresses "hatred" for her (156 [3:201]). Also, as we have discussed in this chapter previously, Hirshl tells Mina about men who feign madness in order to escape marriages or betrothals they did not want. This idea was obviously brewing in Hirshl's mind: try to fake madness and perhaps Mina will leave him for good.

27. It is ironic that Hirshl had risked being labelled a lunatic in order to rid himself of his wife, likely thinking that he would be like those men he told Mina about earlier who feigned madness to get out of matches or marriages they did not want. But in the end this did not get rid of Mina, and in fact he was elevated in stature in the town because of this act. This is due to the fact that his "madness" was interpreted as a ploy to avoid the dreaded draft, and everyone thought he was supremely clever to pull off this ruse. There is a double irony in the fact that if it is true that he faked the madness, he surely did so not to achieve a draft release, but to achieve a marriage release!

28. It could also be that Agnon is suggesting that there is an affinity between authors like himself and psychoanalysts. Both are striving for an understanding of the human psyche or soul. The irony is that the psychoanalyst is given the elevated status of one who can cure people by scientific means, whereas Agnon's portrait of Dr. Langsam humorously shows him doing nothing more than spinning tales.

29. This proverb is one of the most widely quoted of all sayings, and appears in such diverse places as: Aesop's fable of "The Worm and the Fox" (approximately 570 B.C.E.); the New Testament (Luke 4:23); and Rabelais' *Pantagruel,* Book IV, Prologue (1548). Dr. Langsam surely seems to have learned very little from his own life experience. Note that he gives Hirshl his late wife's romantic novels to read, without connecting the fact that perhaps it was these novels that contributed to his wife's romantic escapade with another man and her eventual suicide, as indeed was the case with many who read such novels as Goethe's *The Sorrows of Young Werther.* Moreover, as the subtitle of this chapter implies, I would like to suggest that Agnon's Hirshl is a type of character whose "sorrows" mimic those of Goethe's famous hero, but in a uniquely Jewish and therefore tragicomic way.

30. Dr. Langsam's stories blur the distinction between the premodern traditional Jewish society that was determined by the pious conventions of religious adherence, and the dessicated modern Jewish society of places like Szybusz where the populace has been infected by modern ideas but still clings to

customs it no longer believes in. Therefore, the rosy pictures of life that Dr. Langsam paints have little to do with places like Szybusz, for they obscure the fact that such idyllic societies as he describes may no longer exist.

31. Esther Fuchs makes a similar point about Dr. Langsam's treatment of Hirshl. She calls the treatment Hirshl receives "trivial" and "superficial," dealing only with his physical problems rather than with the deeper causes. See Esther Fuchs, *Omanut ha-hitamemut: 'al ha-'ironiah shel Shai 'Agnon* (Tel Aviv, Israel: University of Tel Aviv, 1985), 96.

32. Dvora Shreibaum devotes a long section in her book on Agnon to an analysis of this dream, which she interprets in distinctly psychoanalytic terms. See *Pesher ha-halomot bi-yetsirotav shel Sh. Y. 'Agnon* (Tel Aviv, Israel: Papyrus, 1993), 273-304.

33. Note that Blume also experienced a nightmare full of potent symbols on the first night she slept at the Hurvitz home. There is in fact a kind of structural parallelism between Hirshl's and Blume's dreams: one begins the novel and the other ends it. There is even a common motif linking the two dreams—the raucous sound of carriage wheels (and crying out but nobody hearing). Both dreams also express deep-seated unhappiness, frustration, and things occurring beyond one's control.

34. It is certainly no accident that immediately prior to the dream, Hirshl had been thinking with contempt about the people of Szybusz, comparing them in his mind to "ants" (192 [3:235-6]). Note that this almost Swiftian depiction of Jewish society in Eastern Europe as "shrunken" or made up of "little people" was commonly used (albeit figuratively) by Yiddish satirists of the nineteenth century. A prime example is Mendele Mocher Seforim's satire *Dos Kleyne Mentshele* (1864).

35. David Aberbach links this blind beggar to one who appears in Flaubert's novel *Madame Bovary* (a connection also made by Robert Alter, *Hebrew and Modernity*, 134-53). Aberbach's point is an interesting one about the possible connection between the two novels. He notes that Emma Bovary encounters a blind beggar precisely when her life is on a downward spiral; he then reappears in a vision just before her death. Aberbach argues that just as the blind beggar represents Emma Bovary's "deterioration," so in Agnon the blind beggar symbolizes Hirshl's "inferiority" and "psychological degradation." See David Aberbach, *At the Handles of the Lock* (New York: Oxford University Press, 1984), 72-3. It should be noted, however, that Flaubert did not create the idea of the blind beggar, for it is a figure derived from folklore. (See Stith Thomson, *Motif Index of Folk Literature*—Motif Number: K1081.1.1.: the tale of the trickster who receives coins from a blind beggar.) Moreover, as Nitza Ben-Dov points out, it is a figure that can also be traced back to one of the tales of Reb Nahman of Bratslav entitled "The Seven Beggars" in which the first beggar who appears in the story happens to be blind. See Ben-Dov, *Ahavot lo me'usharot*, 210. For a good translation and commentary on this tale by Reb Nahman, see Arnold J. Band, ed., *Nahman of Bratslav; The Tales* (New York: Paulist Press, 1978), 253-82; 321-24.

36. See my discussion of this significant point in chapter 3 above.

37. Note that Nitza Ben-Dov devotes almost an entire chapter of her book (chapter 4) to interpreting this dream of Hirshl's. And this she does in distinctly Freudian terms. She sees the cloaked woman in Hirshl's dream as being an image representing both Tsirl *and* Blume; moreover, she states that the dream "expresses Hirshl's wish that the confrontation between the two women should somehow resolve itself" (p. 79). In fact, Ms. Ben-Dov's interpretation of the dream rests on the assumption that the dream is mostly about Tsirl's repressed Oedipal impulses, which express themselves in her "identification as well as rejection" (p. 81) of Blume. As I hope to make clear, my interpretation of the dream is very much unlike this one, for it is my view that the dream should be understood in much simpler terms: as a symbolic tale of Hirshl's failure to accept Blume's love, which had once been his for the taking, much like the piece of cake offered to him in the dream. See Nitza Ben-Dov, *Agnon's Art of Indirection* (Leiden, The Netherlands: E. J. Brill, 1993), 73-106. For a general critique of the Freudian interpretation of *Sipur pashut,* see Hillel Barzel, "Sh. Y. 'Agnon—gilui ve-ne'elam," in *Hikre 'Agnon,* ed. Hillel Weiss and Hillel Barzel (Ramat Gan, Israel: Bar-Ilan University, 1994), 131-75.

38. Refer especially to the scene of Tsirl and Boruch Meir counting their coins at night in their store in a mock-romantic atmosphere. See my chapter 3 above, 64-5.

39. See 64-5 above.

40. Since wild horses are often symbolic of sexual urges, it could be that the danger Blume fears also has to do with the release of her own eros.

41. At one point the narrator even says that life was so good for Hirshl at the sanatorium that "he never had been better off" (188 [3:232]). One could possibly draw a parallel here with Thomas Mann's novel *The Magic Mountain* (1924), in which the patients at the sanatorium are treated so well that most do not want to leave.

42. One could perhaps even argue that this goes against one of the most fundamental tenets of Judaism. In contradistinction to pagan gods, whose worship often entailed the ritual sacrifice of children, the Torah emphasizes how the God of Israel *prevented* Abraham from sacrificing his child Isaac. One could conceivably argue that the sacrifice of the firstborn son in order to achieve "redemption" has some affinity with Christianity, but this certainly could not be applied to Judaism, whose rejection of this idea is at the core of its theology.

43. See my discussion of Hirshl's dream on 91-5 above.

44. Critics are divided on how to interpret the end of the novel. For example, Arnold Band, Hillel Barzel, and Hillel Halkin all see the ending as revealing a basically contented Hirshl, who has learned to accommodate himself to the realities of a less-than-perfect life. Others, such as Gershon Shaked and Nitza Ben-Dov, view the novel's ending as essentially ironic. My reading definitely follows Shaked and Ben-Dov on this point. See Arnold Band, *Nostalgia and Nightmare* (Berkeley: University of California Press, 1968), 239-54; Hillel Barzel, "S. Y. 'Agnon—gilui ve-ne'lam," 152-62; Hillel Halkin, "Afterword" to *A Simple Story* (New York: Schocken, 1985), 231-46; Gershon Shaked, *Shmuel Yosef Agnon: A Revolutionary Traditionalist* (New York: New York University Press, 1989), 130-36; and Nitza Ben-Dov, *Ahavot lo*

me'usharot: tiskul eroti, omanut u-mavet bi-yetsirat 'Agnon (Tel Aviv, Israel: 'Am 'Oved, 1997),'204.

45. Agnon achieves this through his skillful use of irony. As we have discussed earlier in chapter 2 above, this ironic technique is one that Agnon uses throughout the novel. His narrator takes on the voice of the typical inhabitant of the town to describe most of the events that transpire; this is a voice that has the outer sound of piety (e.g., the repetition of the epithet "Elokim ba-shamayim"), but is also scornful and self-righteous in defending the status quo. However, the perceptive reader soon discovers that the events described by the narrator are qualitatively different from how he tries to portray them, thus undermining the reliability of the narrator's pious voice, and deeming his perspective ironic.

46. As Gershon Shaked puts it, "The author does not identify with the victory in the plot. . . . [He] views it as an ironic victory and he condemns it. Thus, the author's attitude is revolutionary—that is, opposed to the plot—and he condemns the victory that he himself arranged." See Gershon Shaked, *Shmuel Yosef Agnon: A Revolutionary Traditionalist*, 136.

47. In this phrase, the translator Hillel Halkin adds the following two words—"to us"—to the English translation, words that actually do not appear in the original Hebrew. Note how the Hebrew reads: "eyn ahava mithaleket le-shnayim. . . . Lo ki, eyla she-hi ba-a im eyn mi she-hotsets beyna u-veyneynu." By adding these two words, the translator gives the line a particular slant that I believe favors a "happy ending" interpretation, since it makes it sound as if Hirshl is talking specifically about himself and Mina. Without these two words, I think that Hirshl's meaning is considerably more ambiguous, and may be even interpreted as referring to himself and Blume Nacht.

48. Note also how this ironic line is followed immediately by a discussion of what happened to Blume Nacht—a kind of "enjambement," linking the implicit subject with the explicit one. Dov Landau points this out as well, citing it as an example within his broad discussion of Agnon's use of juxtapositions. He also uses the rabbinic term—"smikhut parashiot"—to describe this technical literary device. See Dov Landau, *Mi-signon le-mashma'ut be-sipure Shai 'Agnon*, 63-64.

49. On the ending of *Sipur pashut*, see Esther Fuchs, *Omanut ha-hitamemut: 'al ha-'ironiah shel Shai 'Agnon*, 96-97.

50. In his article, "Plot and Denouement in *Sipur Pashut*", A. B. Yehoshua tries to resolve this problem by regarding the abandonment of Meshulam as a "metaphor" that solves "Hirshl's deep psychological problem" (p. 161). Yehoshua interprets Meshulam as "not really a son but a part of Hirshl that was excised from him, that part that prevented him from establishing a true relationship with Mina, that part tied to the mother who neither nurtured nor freed him" (p. 160). Although Yehoshua's reading may be an ingenious way of absolving Hirshl from the "sin" of giving up his own child, I do not believe that the reader would be able to accept it merely on a metaphorical level. Surely, common sense would inform most readers that this is not a portrait of marital bliss at the end of the novel, with the issue of Meshulam's real abandonment standing out as the final issue under discussion between Hirshl and Mina. I think it is fairer to conclude that this is because Agnon would assume there is an instinctive

moral aversion toward the abandonment of one's own child. As a result, Yehoshua's attempt to lift that abandonment onto a metaphorical plane still cannot erase the mark of wrongdoing that would indelibly stain this supposedly happy portrait. See A. B. Yehoshua, "Plot and Denouement in *Sipur Pashut,*" in *Agnon: Texts and Contexts in English Translation,* ed. Leon I. Yudkin (New York: Markus Wiener, 1988), 137-61.

51. Although David Aberbach also interprets the novel as ending with Hirshl's emotional problems "unresolved," he arrives at this conclusion by assessing Hirshl as a typical "schizoid" personality. I believe that this attempt to fit Hirshl into a standard psychoanalytic category misses some of the complexity and subtlety of Agnon's portrait of Hirshl. Although Agnon may well have created a character whose personality traits resemble those of a certain type within psychoanalytic theory, this does not tell the whole story. Agnon surely placed his character within a specific social environment, religious milieu, and historical setting in order to present a multifaceted portrait rather than merely a psychological case study. Aberbach's insights are indeed helpful, but are limited by the parameters to which he conforms. See David Aberbach, *At the Handles of the Lock* (New York: Oxford University Press, 1984), 148.

Chapter 5

Agnon the Theologian: The Crowning Paradox—The Decline of Religion and the Loss of Love

The novel *Sipur pashut* is in no obvious sense a tale about religious life, nor is it a story that primarily concerns itself with theological matters. It is, for all intents and purposes, a story about people who devote very little thought to God and His ways on earth. In fact, to the inhabitants of Szybusz, the earth *is* what counts; those who spend their time on higher things are either foolish, impractical, or both.[1]

At the same time, however, the reader is constantly reminded throughout the novel of the presence of a merciful God. This reminder is issued by the narrator of the story who repeatedly uses the epithet "God in Heaven" (*"Elokim ba-shamayim"*). Significantly, this epithet is used at the very beginning of the novel to justify the death of Mirl, the mother of Blume, whose tragic passing opens the novel, creating an orphan of her daughter. But, strangely enough, Mirl's death as conveyed by the narrator is represented as a kind of "blessing" from God because, according to him, God had put an end to Mirl's many years of suffering by finally taking her from this world (3 [3:55]).

An astute reader would surely ask: what should one make of this God who causes tragic events such as this to occur, but is then lauded for His true mercy behind such acts? Should the reader be skeptical about such mercy, or should he suspect the *conveyer* of such statements to be harboring disingenuous motives? In other words, why does Agnon use the services of a pious narrator, and then proceed to undermine that very piety by the story this narrator tells?[2]

The disparity between the narrative voice and the story that is told by it is certainly not a new fictive technique.[3] What is unique in this novel, however, is the *subtlety* of the clash between what is uttered by the narrator and what is shown to happen in the novel. This makes it oftentimes difficult for the reader to discern whether the narrator is in accord with the society that he describes, or whether he is actually mocking it. For example, the narrator takes on the voice of the typical "pious" inhabitant of Szybusz. But although the reader soon discovers that the townsfolk have lost most of their internal piety, they do still retain its external forms. Even the novel's main character, Hirshl Hurvitz, does not stray far from the path laid out for him by the dictates of his religious upbringing, despite the fact that his thoughts wander perilously close to the edge.

On the one hand, this disparity might be interpreted as follows: that the novel is written as a kind of subtle condemnation of present-day life that has drawn modern Jews away from the sanctity of their traditional faith. On the other hand, it could also be implying the exact opposite: that the novel seeks to convey how the tired old habits of religious life are so ingrained in the Jews that nothing short of a revolution could force them to finally cast off the last vestiges of their "stultifying" religion. Whether the former or the latter interpretation is espoused (and we shall make that judgment in due course), it is nonetheless clear from the very beginning of the novel that Agnon creates a kind of religious veneer or "overlay" in which the narrator and the characters render lip service to the right pieties and rituals, but are shown through the significant details of the text to have lost all true belief.[4] Surely this is one of the chief ironies of this portrait of Szybusz, influencing to one degree or another everything that occurs in the story.

It is only logical, then, that the love story of Hirshl Hurvitz and Blume Nacht would also be affected by the societally sanctioned banality of religious life in Szybusz. But like all else in this novel, the disparity between traditional obedience and modern freedom is often blurred by Agnon's subtle ironic style, leaving it to the perspicacious reader to uncover whether religion is a force for the better or for the worse within the sanctimonious confines of Szybusz life. Certainly regarding the problem of love, the question must be asked: if Szybusz had been able to sustain true piety among its inhabitants, would the love story of Hirshl and Blume have been more likely to have had a happy ending? Or, is Agnon suggesting that what is needed is a *complete* overthrow of religion and its "debilitating" influence in order to endow Jews such as Hirshl with the independence and strength to claim love for themselves at last?

It is no easy task to understand the role of religion in the novel, since religious inferences are scattered throughout many segments of the plot in a seemingly offhand fashion. Among these inferences, however, are a number of hints about the *past* state of religious life in Szybusz,[5] showing that religion had once assumed a vital presence in the town even among those who embraced "enlightened" ideas. Such pious devotion to religion has all but disappeared in present-day Szybusz, where the attitude toward Jewish belief and practice has become strangely ambivalent. This sharp contrast between past and present religious life in the town is summed up in the following reflection by the narrator:

> there was a tradition of high-minded inquiry going back to the days when pious Jews with an interest in worldly knowledge still had more piety than worldliness—that is, to those Bible critics and grammarians of the last century who, when they prayed, made sure to pronounce every letter of the ancient Hebrew correctly and not like most Jews who swallow all their words until the angels themselves cannot make head or tail of them. (37 [3:86])

But what caused religion to go into decline and lose the intense intellectual and spiritual loyalty of its adherents? The answer in this novel seems to lie in the *embourgeoisement* of the population. With the growth of the Jewish middle class and its emphasis on worldly success, religion like everything else is now measured according to its usefulness as a *commodity*.[6] On this note, it is surely significant that virtually the only rabbi to appear in the novel is Rabbi Zanvil, a fellow patient of Hirshl's in the sanatorium (185,

188 [3:228-9; 3:231-2]). Rabbi Zanvil is sent to the sanatorium because he is convinced that he is dead. Although his community
deems him mad, the perceptive reader can see that Rabbi Zanvil's
"delusions" are not so far off the mark: he *is* dead in the sense that
he is an anachronism. Religion has become so superfluous that
rabbis are now expendable. Hence Agnon takes Nietzsche's maxim
that "God is dead" one step further, showing that if religion becomes meaningless to a society, then its practitioners, like Rabbi
Zanvil, become corpselike relics of an obsolete time.[7]

How appropriate, then, that not only are there no other rabbis
in the novel, but there is no one who even aspires to become one!
Indeed, Hirshl's mother Tsirl, who epitomizes the base materialism
of the new Szybusz middle class, is secretly relieved when her son
gives up his rabbinic aspirations. As Tsirl puts it, "Of course there
were rabbis who earned handsome livings too, but how many of
them could you point to? Not even one per town, whereas the
goods of a merchant were always in demand" (15 [3:66]).[8]

The fact that religious life, formerly the highest aspiration of
the Jews of Szybusz,[9] has been reduced to a mere commodity of
little practical value, is a highly revealing statement about the
paucity of spiritual values in general within the community, a
paucity no doubt with far-ranging implications.[10] As is demon-
strated by the severe social limitations imposed upon Hirshl
Hurvitz, the lack of any ideal in the society other than that of material prosperity engenders a kind of dullness among the populace,
to whom aspirations of a higher nature are barely conceivable.
Therefore heroism is absent in Szybusz, as is passion in general. At
least in the past when religion was alive in Szybusz, there was a
kind of religious passion that existed among the pious population.
Heroism may not have taken the form of warring knights and rescued maidens, but there existed another type of hero among the
Jewish populace whose commitment was to a higher calling, i.e.,
scholars and saints devoted to their almighty God.[11]

Alas, no such heroes exist now in Szybusz, for materialism has
reduced the formally religious society to the lowest common de-
nominator, somehow yielding a pernicious mixture of crudeness
and levity in the townsfolk. A perfect example of this phenomenon
is the scene of the Chanukah party at the home of the Gildenhorns,

where Hirshl becomes accidentally engaged to Mina. The target of many of the jokes at this party is religion, specifically the traditions of Judaism and its lore, even though these jokes are often told indirectly through parody or sarcasm rather than through direct criticism. For example, when Yitzhok Gildenhorn congratulates Hirshl on his engagement to Mina, he says in German "*Ich gratuliere,*" rather than the traditional Jewish phrase *mazel tov*. The narrator then proceeds to comment on this phrase as follows, "Saying *ich gratuliere*, to be sure, was not quite the same as saying *mazel tov* to a groom. It was more like something one might say to the winner of a card game" (59-60 [3:108]). The narrator's droll comment points out something crucial about Gildenhorn's choice of words far beyond their apparent tactlessness. It shows how far removed the Szybusz Jews are from the sanctity of their religious rituals, so that even an event such as a marriage betrothal receives no more reverence than the winning of a game of pinochle.[12]

Later in the evening, in the midst of drinking and revelry, the religious texts then become the focus of parody. For example, one of the revelers breaks into a drunken rendition of the Sabbath prayer *Eyshet hayil* ("Woman of Valor") taken from Proverbs 31:10-31, obviously making fun of the religious respect bestowed upon wives by traditional Jewish husbands (66 [3:114]). Also, when the bride is about to be toasted, one of the drunken guests responds with the following twist on the well-known psalm of exile, Psalm 137: "May my drinking hand wither," said Mottshi Shaynbart, "if I didn't think of suggesting that long ago" (65 [3:114]). Transforming the psalm into a subject of parody not only betrays the irreverence of the character who uttered it, but also reveals how distant the Jew in this novel is from the sentiment of the psalm itself. Indeed, how ironic it is that the original psalm, which pledges never to forget Jerusalem, is now uttered by one who seems to care little about spiritual matters, preferring instead to place drink, instead of Jerusalem, above his "chiefest joy."[13]

The only character in the novel who *does* seem to show concern for God and His ways on earth is Mina's father, Gedalia Ziemlich. The problem with Gedalia, however, is that his "religiosity" verges on the paranoic: it consists of constantly fretting and worrying that all his wealth and good fortune in life will at any moment be taken away from him by God (87-91 [3:135-8]; 116 [3:163]). Nervous and anxiety-ridden, Gedalia Ziemlich performs his religious duties to a fault, but they seem to be done more to appease a "jealous" deity who Gedalia fears might begrudge him too much happiness, rather than because of any sublime faith in the gracious and yet mysterious goodness of God.[14] Gedalia Ziemlich's approach to religion is confounding, not only because of his evident lack of faith in God's mercy, but also because of what it shows in general about the so-called religious Jew in this society. In Agnon's portrait, the Jewish religion has become the province of the weak and fearful, who hang onto their religion as a kind of temporary hedge against impending misfortune, not unlike primitive tribesmen clinging to superstition.[15] It follows then that the strength and courage that once ensued from belief in the God of Israel clearly have no place in the vocabulary of faith of Gedalia Ziemlich and his kind. Indeed, if Gedalia Ziemlich is any proof, the word "religion" in this novel connotes a strange mixture of anxious appeasement and morbid dread.

Another key example of how religious belief in Szybusz society verges on superstition is the primitive beliefs that are held by Hirshl's mother Tsirl. Convinced that her family is under a curse of madness that was laid upon them generations ago, Tsirl had hoped that Hirshl would become a rabbi in order to atone for the "sin" that originally brought the curse upon the family. (Her great-great grandfather once insulted a rabbi by remarking that the rabbi appeared to be going out of his mind due to an excess of piety; the rabbi responded by saying that if anyone is going out of his mind, it is this man and his descendants.)[16] The fact that Tsirl wanted Hirshl to be a rabbi in order to avoid the family curse, rather than because she considered the rabbinical vocation to be *in and of itself* one of the highest callings, is indicative of how low religion has sunk in the eyes of the populace. But, as pointed out earlier, when Hirshl loses interest in his rabbinical studies and comes to work in the store, Tsirl seems to heave a quiet sigh of relief. Perhaps believing that she has "sidetracked" the curse by leading Hirshl—at least for a while—in the direction of a religious vocation, Tsirl seems to rest satisfied that she has done her part to appease the "dark forces," while at the same time ensuring a good income for her son in the family business![17]

It could be argued, however, that the degenerated "religious" mentality exemplified by Gedalia Ziemlich and Tsirl Hurvitz has no *necessary* bearing on the life of our hero, Hirshl Hurvitz, except for one inescapable fact: Hirshl's tacit acceptance of all his society's values, so much so that he chooses to feign lunacy rather than simply reject those norms. In fact, it could even be counterargued that Hirshl embodies the "spiritual" problems of modern *galut* society as Agnon perceived it, his madness being a symbolic representation of the self-destructive tendency within this type of Jewish community.[18] If so, then religion as a central force within this environment must be understood in terms of its effect upon Hirshl as both a character within the novel's plot, and as a symbolic representative of the spiritual condition of the modern *galut* Jew.

Certainly, when it comes to religion, Hirshl is typical of the nominally pious Jew of Szybusz. He performs the required rituals, and participates in the holiday observances, but rarely displays any keen interest in the deeper significance of such acts. But beyond this, there seems to be no *obvious* connection between the incidental religiosity of Hirshl and the obsessive piety of Gedalia Ziemlich. However, though not overtly similar, there is something uncannily alike in their underlying modes of thinking. For Gedalia, religion serves as a kind of hovering dark omnipresence—warning, threatening, and poised to strike; if the worst should occur, the only thing to do is to passively accept it as a kind of divine ordinance.[19] Hirshl's mentality is similarly slavish: though not concerned with divine punishment, he too always fears the worst; thus for him the best route is always the one that is the safest (and most passive) one. That is to say, Hirshl may not display the same religious dread as does Gedalia Ziemlich, whose degenerated pietism verges on the paranoic, but it is dread nonetheless that Hirshl emits. Stripped of its religious underpinnings, Hirshl's perpetual anxiety is expressed in secularized and psychological terms, even as it is conveyed ironically through the "naive" observations of the narrator.

Indeed, the languid passivity that seems to go hand in hand with Hirshl's dread of catastrophe at times even takes on a

"mythic" cast within the novel. For example, when Hirshl's accidental engagement to Mina is declared by the guests at the Gildenhorn party, rather than speaking up and correcting the mistake,
Hirshl is distracted by the memory of a mythic tale he once heard
as a child (and with which he now clearly identifies):

> Hirshl sat wondering what he was doing there. He felt dazed
> and dejected. Several times he tried thinking things through
> and gave up. His mind kept jumping until it settled on a story
> he once was told as a child about a man who, finding himself
> at a wedding, suddenly noticed that the bride and groom were
> made of straw, that the guests were all trolls, and that every-
> thing in the house was an enchantment. Just as he was about
> to flee for dear life he saw that the wedding ring was real gold
> and decided to take it. No sooner had he done so than the
> bride stuck out a finger and he slipped the golden ring onto it.
> The trolls roared with laughter and so did he. His new wife
> seized him by his jacket tails and never let go of him again.
> (61-62 [3:110])

What does this tale of the man and the trolls tell us about Hirshl
and his reluctance to stop the engagement process before it is too
late? It is not difficult to extrapolate from what happens to the man
in the tale why in his own life Hirshl's attitude toward *his* "straw
bride"[20] is so utterly passive. As this tale indicates, Hirshl seems to
believe that once an event has occurred, there is nothing that can be
done to change it. In other words, as such ancient pagan myths
expound, one is trapped by one's fate, and there is no turning back.
Surprisingly, the notion of free will that is so integral to traditional
Jewish thinking seems to be a foreign notion to Hirshl, and hardly
crosses his mind as a genuine possibility for his own life.[21]

It should also be noted that what is particularly curious about
the mythic tale of the man and the trolls is the fact that when the
trolls roar with laughter after the man is trapped by the bride, the
man laughs along *with* them. This reveals the utter foolhardiness of
the man himself, who apparently does not realize that the trolls are
laughing at him. Moreover, it also shows how pathetic he is to accept the will of a community of trolls—dwarf-like creatures in both
body and soul—whose parallel to the small-minded residents of
Szybusz is obvious.

If this mixture of foolishness and fatalism truly reflects the mentality of our hero Hirshl Hurvitz (the modern Jewish *everyman* in Agnon's fictional vision), surely one is moved to ask whether there is anyone at all in Szybusz who maintains the indigenous Jewish religious wisdom that had once been rigorously preserved by centuries of diaspora Jews. Certainly the other characters in the novel do not seem to embody such wisdom, and as the little mythic tale illustrates, are themselves rather troll-like in character—mean in spirit and quick to trap.[22] From the perspective of this novel, the answer to this question becomes tragically clear: that Judaism as a source of traditional wisdom seems to have all but disappeared from towns like Szybusz. Even two of the most earnest Jews in the novel—the punishment-obsessed Gedalia Ziemlich and the self-absorbed Hirshl Hurvitz—believe in a form of "religion" that is closer to Greek tragedy than it is to Jewish justice. Indeed, as Agnon shows in this work, Judaism has become dormant in the minds and hearts of Szybusz's Jewish populace, to the extent that nothing short of a revolution will serve to rouse its sleeping regiments.

The question remains, however: what brought about this dormancy? Although Agnon does not attempt to explain the vicissitudes of modern Jewish religious history within the context of this novel, he does nevertheless offer the reader sufficient clues to allow for a fairly clear picture to emerge. First, we begin to perceive that the neglect of the religious tradition seems to be tied to an intense desire to forget the oppressive historical and political conditions of Jewish life in the past. To be sure, the description in the novel of what life had been like for the Jews of Szybusz is a devastating one, full of tales of persecution and torment at the hands of the gentiles—everything from a synagogue burning (138 [3:184]) to the intentional drowning of a wagon load of Jews (139 [3:185]). But it seems that in their overzealous desire to forget such bitter memories, the Jews of Szybusz not only abandoned their old *physical* neighborhood (the Jewish Quarter), but they also abandoned their *spiritual* home. Judaism, once the highest source of scholarship and inspiration, has become linked in their minds to images of a horrific past, fraught with misery and servitude. Now left behind along with the empty stores and houses, the Jewish religion has become as deeply buried as the graves lying beneath the pavement stones, forlorn and forgotten in the old abandoned Jewish Quarter of Szybusz.[23]

Significantly, it is to this old Jewish Quarter that Hirshl Hurvitz ventures on his nightly wanderings, struggling to overcome his insomnia and his marital woes. But it is not a fascination with past Jewish history and religion that draws Hirshl to this neighborhood; the fact that Blume Nacht lives here is enough motivation alone to lead him here on regular pilgrimages, in the hope that she will catch sight of him and presumably save him from his unhappy life with Mina. However, one might ask whether Agnon is also intimating that Hirshl is unconsciously undergoing a type of spiritual transformation by returning to the place where his ancestors lived and died. Unfortunately, the answer must be negative. And lest the reader be tempted to interpret it in this fashion, the narrator lets the reader know in no uncertain terms that although Hirshl has the potential to be moved by his ancestral surroundings,[24] they barely have any effect upon him. As the narrator bluntly describes Hirshl: "He was not, after all, a chronicler of human misery, which was something he gladly left to Akavia Mazal, in whose house Blume lived" (140 [3:185]).

It is clear that Hirshl, like most of the other Jews of Szybusz, wishes to forget the gloomy past and all that goes with it. But, as Agnon shows in the novel, just because the oppression of the Jews has lessened, this does not mean they are free of it. As we are repeatedly shown, the bribing of gentile officials is an ongoing fact of Jewish existence in Szybusz and other such towns. Even the relative freedom from persecution that the Jews do enjoy must be seen as a questionable form of freedom,[25] for it is based on a forgetfulness of their own past sufferings, and a denial of all they had once sacrificed themselves for, and which now they have lost in the process of forgetting. In other words, if Hirshl (or anyone else in Agnon's Szybusz) were to look honestly at modern Jewish existence in towns like Szybusz, they would have to see it as part of a continuum with the past. Indeed, it could be said that the refusal to judge the present in terms of the past locks them in a kind of hellish present. Unable to look back, they can neither recover the good things they have given up, nor detect whether the evils of the past are about to be repeated in the future.[26]

True freedom, i.e., the freedom that comes with an understanding of the past both personal and historical, is something that Hirshl desperately lacks, as do most of the other members of Szybusz society.[27] How appropriate it is then that the only one who does seem to possess such freedom is the scholar Akavia Mazal, whose life's work it is to study the past. Unconcerned about what people think, he freely chooses to live apart from the bulk of Jews in Szybusz, pursuing an unconventional career in historical scholarship. Significantly, his scholarship is centered on the history of Jewish life in Szybusz, so despite Mazal's isolation from the present Szybusz community—and perhaps *because* of it—it could be interpreted that Mazal is closer to the essence of Jewish Szybusz than the very people who are its descendants and "heirs."[28]

It is surely no coincidence that Akavia Mazal is also the only one in the novel who is shown to have married for love. The relationship between freedom and love is an integral one, for it seems that along with the freedom that comes with a realistic and clear-eyed understanding of the past, there is an added benefit: a deepened understanding of the kind of life one wants to live in the present as an *individual*. This of course includes who one chooses to marry.[29] In this light, it also makes sense that Blume Nacht ends up working for the Mazal family and residing with them, for like both Akavia and Tirza Mazal, Blume too is one who chooses the way she wants to live independent of societal norms. As a result, Blume does not succumb to the attentions of suitors such as Getzel Stein or Dr. Knabenhut, preferring instead to remain a spinster rather than submit to societal pressure and get married to the first man who shows an interest in her.[30]

Akavia Mazal, however, is not the only character in the novel who is interested in the Jewish past.[31] The neurologist Dr. Langsam, to whom Hirshl is sent following his "mad" episode in the forest, is someone who thinks about the past almost obsessively. But the type of reflections on past Jewish life in which Dr. Langsam indulges are significantly different from those of Akavia Mazal, because they focus only on the good and exclude anything negative from their field of vision. In this way, his memories are closer to what can be termed nostalgia than to historical under-standing. Indeed, Dr. Langsam's tales with which he regales Hirshl are all stories that romanticize the town of his childhood. He de-scribes Jews who, despite their abject poverty, lived lives of saintly simplicity. He especially admired his local rabbi whose sole possession was a goose quill that he used in order to write annota-tions on religious texts; his utter simplicity was such that when his quill broke, he would use his fingernail to mark his comments in the text.

Although Dr. Langsam's idyllic stories possess a certain degree of charm in their appreciation of the religious virtues of premodern Jewish society, at the same time there is something odd about the fact that Dr. Langsam seems totally unaware of the political vul-nerability of such communities. From the narrator's discussion of Akavia Mazal and his scholarly research on the history of Szy-busz, the reader has already been made aware of some of the hor-rors experienced by Jews in recent centuries. How could Dr. Langsam, a man of worldly experience and knowledge, not be aware of such facts? Could it be a type of conscious blindness on his part? Indeed, this seems to be the case.[32] In fact, it can be argued that this blindness to the realities of past Jewish life is symp-tomatic of Dr. Langsam's general malaise, in which he apparently chooses to know only about that which is pleasant. The problem with that kind of selective memory is that the truth becomes what-ever one wants it to be, leaving one in a state of perpetual ignorance even in the face of the most obvious facts that are apparent for ev-eryone to see.

This perhaps explains why Dr. Langsam could not prevent the disaster that occurred in his own personal life, the facts of which are particularly grim. As the reader learns from the narrator, Dr. Langsam's wife had taken her own life following an unhappy adul-terous love affair with a local "Don Juan" (191 [3:234]). Is this meant to suggest that there is some connection between Dr. Langsam's Pollyanna-like approach to life and his failure in matters of the heart? Agnon may in fact be suggesting this very thing. Just as Akavia Mazal's "realism" seems to go hand in hand with his personal happiness, so in a kind of opposite sense does Dr. Langsam's "romanticism" seem to lead to his own *un*happiness.

Indeed, Dr. Langsam may be seen as a kind of "tragic-romantic" prototype in Agnon's cast of characters.[33] Pining for the glories of the past, Langsam is typical of the romantic dreamer who prefers the unattainable (and the past, by its very nature, is doubtlessly irretrievable) than that which he actually possesses. Thus, it is not unreasonable to assume that Dr. Langsam's wife became a victim of neglect at the hands of her husband, who clearly lives more in the past than in the present. Perhaps it is no wonder that his wife became unfaithful and eventually despaired of the world. Whatever the facts behind it, even her death has a kind of quasi-romantic quality to it—a veritable Madame Bovary!—giving the doctor even more reason to view himself in a tragic-romantic light. Moreover, Dr. Langsam seems unable to learn anything from the personal failures of his own recent past: he gives Hirshl his late wife's romantic novels to read, without seeming to realize that there may be a causal connection between these melodramas and his wife's erratic behavior, dismissing these books as simply containing "a lot of descriptions of ladies' fashions" (190 [3:234]).[34]

Hence, the blindness of the romantic who lives for the past but can learn none of its lessons is well satirized in the figure of Dr. Langsam. His name, meaning "slow" in German, can give way to many humorous interpretations, an obvious one being "slow-witted." Although some interpreters have seen Dr. Langsam as a serious and even admirable figure who teaches Hirshl to appreciate the beauty of bygone days,[35] it seems clear that this is a clever trap set by Agnon to taunt those romantically-inclined readers who jump at the chance to find a kindred spirit in literature. A word to the wise here is in order: in Hirshl's entire course of treatment at the sanatorium, he is never once asked by Dr. Langsam to speak about what is troubling him, but rather it is Hirshl who sits and listens to the old doctor speaking about himself and spinning tales about *his* past. The inherent humor in this reversal of roles notwithstanding, there is something strangely suspect about playing the role of doctor and never even examining your patient. Is it any wonder then that Hirshl's "cure" at the hands of Dr. Langsam is such a sham that he eventually returns to Szybusz the same deeply troubled young man as he started out? Hirshl goes through no true rite of passage or process of enlightenment, and comes no closer to achieving a *bildung* than he was at the beginning of the novel—not as one would expect in a true novel of the education of the hero, in which life "instructs" the move from innocence to experience. At the end of the novel he is still the same Hirshl Hurvitz as he was at the outset: fretful, childish, and utterly confused about himself as well as about the nature of love.

Could it be drawn from Hirshl's experience at the sanatorium that his failure to grow as an individual, and his consequent emotional immaturity regarding women, has much to do with his continued dependence on religion, something which has only been intensified during his stay at the sanatorium thanks to Dr. Langsam's sugar-coated tales of past Jewish religious life? Although it may be tempting to follow this line of argument, religion is actually an unlikely source of Hirshl's problems since he maintains few ties to religious life, and those that he does are merely ritual in nature. In this way Hirshl is similar to most other members of Szybusz society for whom religion holds little spiritual value and hence is in a state of general decline. Indeed, freedom *from* religion seems to operate de facto in Szybusz, as everyone seems to acknowledge "with a wink." In other words, religion in Szybusz is practically an empty shell, with no power left either to uplift the human spirit, or even to suppress it.

One might then ask: without religion to bind him, why is Hirshl not free to pursue his desires? It is significant to note that while many of Agnon's predecessors and contemporaries had striven to portray the loss of religion as a "liberating force," Agnon's novel shows something quite different. In fact, in *Sipur pashut* the decline of religion in Szybusz has not endowed its residents with much freedom of spirit at all. Not only do Agnon's characters lack the will to develop their own individuality, but they also refrain from pursuing deep relationships based on personal choice. If religion had ever deprived them of their ability to love, then the loss of it has not liberated them from that ineptitude.

Can it be concluded, then, that religion has little to do with Hirshl's lack of independence in matters of the heart? Before attempting to answer this conclusively, it might be useful to place this question in its larger context. This is because it may be the case that the accepted Enlightenment idea of individual freedom, arising as a natural consequence of shaking off the shackles of religion, is an assumption that cannot simply be applied to the Jews. For one thing, it may be argued that the Jewish religion is by nature less restrictive in regard to matters of individual freedom, especially in the areas of love and sex. While Christian theology stresses fundamental notions such as "original sin" and "redemption through suffering," Judaism does not define itself through such ascetic concepts. This does not mean to say that premodern Judaism adopts a lenient view toward courtship and sexual freedom, for it has undoubtedly woven strict rules regulating such matters into its legal codes. But Judaism traditionally balances such stringent rules with an equally strong endorsement of marriage and "fruitfulness" as commandments that the dutiful Jew follows in order to honor God. This makes it dubious, therefore, as to whether Judaism is or has ever been as restrictive as Christianity in regard to male-female relationships, especially in terms of its general attitude and approach. As a result, modern Jewish literature, unlike modern European literature in general, did not need to portray such an extreme rejection of religion in order to embrace the modern ideal of romantic love, especially insofar as it bears on matters of sex. Indeed, such matters are not in dispute in Agnon's *Sipur pashut*; it is scarcely the traditional religious authorities, or even traditional religious opinions internalized by Hirshl, that stand in the way of his love for Blume.

Alternatively, even if one were to argue that when it comes to *eros* Judaism is almost as emotionally restrictive as Christianity is repressive, it is nevertheless still questionable whether in Agnon's mind the discarding of religion would serve to liberate the Jew in matters of the heart, as advocates of the Enlightenment have generally proposed. In *Sipur pashut,* Agnon portrays this problem in all its complexity through the character of Hirshl Hurvitz who, despite the loss of religious piety, is still a man without freedom. That is to say, Hirshl has left the *Bayt Midrash* (Study House) both physically and spiritually, but he has not become a transformed individual as a result of this departure. Thus, implicit in Agnon's portrait of Hirshl lies the question: what real freedom—whether romantic or individual—has been gained from "emancipation" by Jews such as Hirshl Hurvitz?

Agnon's novel shows that the loss of religion in modern Szybusz has not led to a net gain in freedom, nor has it engendered a veritable flowering of romantic love, as was supposed to happen according to the promise of the Enlightenment.[36] Indeed, the crowning paradox of the novel lies in the fact that although the modern diaspora Jew such as Hirshl may be free in the *external* sense of having achieved economic prosperity and some degree of societal acceptance, the accompanying loss of religion in the modern world makes him actually less free in the *inner* or *spiritual* sense, and thus less able to love.[37] This does not mean to suggest that the Jews in premodern society were free to embrace ideas of romantic love and individual choice. On the contrary, the arranged marriage was a staple of their civilization. Yet premodern Jewish society possessed a kind of wholeness, even if it lacked romance, endowing the Jew with a sure and confident knowledge of his place in the world. This all changed, however, once the harbingers of the Enlightenment ushered in new concepts of individual rights and desires, and thereby introduced romantic love into the arena of modern Jewish life. And once the floodgates of romantic expectation had been opened there was no quelling the tide. The problem is that the infusion of romantic expectation into Jewish society was not, as Agnon shows, a simple story. Love and freedom, the natural corollaries, are still at odds with one another. If traditional religion had once provided the Jews with a solid grounding for their identity—in self-knowledge and pride as Jews—then the loss of it has not brought about freedom but insecurity. This is apparent in Jews like Hirshl Hurvitz who lack the inner freedom once granted by religion, and who now exist in a kind of religious "no-man's-land": they possess neither the solid religious identity of bygone days nor the liberating benefits that might come from a true secular revolt.

The fundamental question as to *why* Hirshl is unable to achieve the necessary individual freedom that would enable him to love is something that Agnon only hints at. But by putting all of Agnon's hints together, one is able to form a fairly clear idea of what he is ultimately suggesting: it is not religion that is the great debilitating force in Jewish life, but it is the lack of *political* freedom that is eating away at the soul of Jewish society. This is why Agnon would not be advocating any kind of return to a pre-Enlightenment religious society for Jews in the *galut,* despite his obvious respect for the integrity of that earlier civilization.[38] Agnon's awareness of the precariousness of the modern Jew in eastern European society (especially by 1935) is in fact a kind of subtext that underlies the entire novel, but it is presented in such an incidental and seemingly haphazard way that one could easily overlook it.[39] This is partly to do with the fact that the characters themselves do not wish to take seriously the external threats to their existence, and instead like to pride themselves on being Jews living in "modern times" where such dangers do not apply to *them,* but rather are a thing of the past. The perceptive reader, however, can surely detect more than a touch of self-delusion at work here, for there are many deliberate references to the political vulnerability of the Jews spread throughout the novel. For example, the fact that Jewish boys like Hirshl are desperately trying to avoid the draft is not necessarily because of any innate lack of courage on their part, but rather (as it is implied in the novel) it is because they are being singled out *as Jews* to fight on the front lines, and thus would inevitably be the first soldiers to be killed (133 [3:179]). There are also numerous references in the novel showing the Jews of Szybusz still needing to bribe gentile officials in order to ensure that they remain in their good graces (139, etc. [3:185]). Moreover, there is even a rumor in the novel of Jewish girls being "waylaid" and enticed into convents by Catholic priests (209 [3:251]).

If, as Agnon's portrait shows, the Jews of Szybusz are in fact living in a menacing environment, it is no wonder then that achieving freedom and "normalcy" both as individuals and as a society remains a difficult and ever-receding goal.[40] That would also explain why giving up religion does not free such Jews, because it is not religion that is the root cause of their abnormal state. Of course, it had been argued (especially by socialists) that stripping the Jews of their religion is the first step toward liberating them politically, since the Jewish religion at the time no doubt encouraged the passive acceptance of their fate in the *galut.* But as Agnon shows in his novel, the loss of religion seems to have only led to a dead end, because while it stripped the Jew of his uniqueness, it did not *necessarily* endow him with political courage.

Thus, we see in Szybusz the results of a religion-less Judaism: a society of spineless individuals who join national-political movements only in order to use them as recreational facilities and *not* in order to effect real change.[41] Of course, part of this political lethargy stems from the simple fact that nationalism alone outside of one's homeland generally rests on thin ground. But in the case of the Szybusz Jew, the situation is made worse by the fact that he *thinks* he is free, and hence for him nationalism has little urgency.[42] Indeed as Agnon's portrait shows, such a Jew is doubly bereft, for not only has he surrendered his religious integrity as a member of an ancient and unique people, but he has gained nothing in return for doing so. Moreover, the irony of it all is that he does not even know it![43]

Hence Jews such as Hirshl Hurvitz have little chance of achieving independence so long as they remain within Szybusz society, due to the layers of deception upon which their so-called modern society is built. Therefore, nothing that Hirshl does in the novel is able to free him from his personal problems because the problems are larger than himself, and his family, and even his particular town. Freedom for a Jew such as Hirshl would require a clear-eyed assessment of the political realities of being a Jew in eastern Europe, without lies and without sentiment. It would also require an objective critique of the type of *people* which that society produces (those like himself!), as well as the courage to face the shameful truth about his own weakness. Perhaps only then would characters like Hirshl Hurvitz have the chance at a *new* life—probably far away from Szybusz or anything resembling it. And only then would they marry the girls they love, thereby creating the love stories that are, it would seem for Agnon, surely the mark of all healthy and free societies.

Notes

1. Baruch Kurzweil lays stress on the point that religious life in Szybusz is devoid of humanity, especially in its lack of pity for the poor and the suffering. See Baruch Kurzweil, *Masot 'al sipure Shai 'Agnon* (Tel Aviv, Israel: Schocken, 1970), 354.

2. Gershon Shaked poses similar questions in his discussion of the ironic stance of the narrator. See Gershon Shaked, "Bat ha-melekh ve-se'udat ha-'em," in *Omanut ha-sipur shel 'Agnon* (Tel Aviv, Israel: Sifri'at Poalim, 1973), 211. Esther Fuchs takes Shaked's position one step further by arguing that ultimately the writer of *Sipur pashut* is mocking the perspective of his own narrator, whom he portrays as being sunk in the mire of his society. See Esther Fuchs, *Omanut ha-hitamemut: 'al ha-'ironia shel Shai 'Agnon* (Tel Aviv, Israel: Tel Aviv University Press, 1985), 56-8.

3. See Wayne Booth, *The Rhetoric of Fiction* (Chicago: University of Chicago Press, 1961), 316-23.

4. Note that there are times when the narrator himself "lets down his guard" and conveys attitudes toward the Jewish religion that are far removed from his usual pious tone. A good example of this occurs in the discussion of the many newspapers that are now available in Szybusz (211 [3:253]). The narrator ironically expresses awe for the amount of knowledge one can quickly acquire from reading newspapers, and contrasts this with the hours spent (and "wasted") by previous generations on Talmud study. As he not so subtly puts it, "what had they [the Talmud scholars] known in the end? A whole lot of fairy tales, whereas after an hour of reading the newspaper one was an encyclopedia on two legs oneself" (211 [3:253]).

5. Kurzweil makes the pointed observation that Agnon's critical depiction of the *present* state of Jewish religious life is largely achieved through his contrasting it with the idealized religious life of the *past,* an ironic technique that Kurzweil sees in almost all of Agnon's works. See Baruch Kurzweil, "Ha-yesod ha-dati be-kitve 'Agnon," in *Masot 'al Sipure Shai 'Agnon* (Tel Aviv, Israel: Schocken, 1970), 328-52, especially 335.

6. The narrator makes it clear that Hirshl's study of the holy texts was abandoned on the very day that he began to work in the store of his parents. The reader learns this toward the middle of the novel, in the scene where Hirshl returns after a long absence to the study house: he opens a folio of the Talmud and notices a folded page, recognizing it as the page that he had folded on the very day he went to work at the shop, and therefore the last day he had ever opened a text of Talmud (16 [3:67]). Not only does he find he can no longer read the text, but he remembers that he had once been so adept at it that "no intricacy of the passage would have escaped him." Now he sees that he cannot even remember the meaning of the Aramaic words (154 [3:199]).

7. Note that Hirshl is struck by the utter beauty of the stories that Rabbi Zanvil tells him about Jewish religious life in the past, a religious life that is now all but dead—hence the term "necrologies" used by the narrator to describe such tales. Thus the narrator describes Hirshl's awestruck response, "Hirshl had

never heard such wonderful stories in his life, every one of them brimming with the love of God and His chosen people" (188 [3:232]).

8. Tsirl's attitude toward religion did not arise out of a vacuum. Her father also seems to have had a certain degree of contempt for religion, especially as compared to what he viewed as the more serious business of life—running a store. In a perverse comparison of the two, he was known to have said, "a store was not a synagogue in which to sit around and gab" (85-6 [3:133]).

9. Note the former glory of the Great Synagogue of the town, with its elaborate artwork found within, testifying to the respect and awe it once generated among its adherents (14-15 [3:65]).

10. The respect for traditional religious life is a distinguishing feature of Agnon's writing. In fact, Meshulam Tochner views it as one of the prominent features of Agnon's work, especially in comparison with that of most other modern Hebrew writers who put much less emphasis upon it. See Meshulam Tochner, *Pesher Agnon* (Tel Aviv, Israel: Masada, 1968), 227-31.

11. The *lack* of any truly pious characters in the novel is noteworthy. The only exception may be Blume's father, Hayyim Nacht, even though within Szybusz and its environs he was given no respect; he was even spurned as a kind of ne'er-do-well because of his lack of worldly success (19-22 [3:69-72]). Cf. also chapter 2, above (39-40), for a fuller discussion of Hayyim Nacht and his role in the novel.

12. Note the irony in the fact that this is ostensibly *Chanukah* that is being celebrated, i.e., a time when Judaism as a religion is traditionally celebrated for having heroically defended itself against enforced pagan ritual. Here, of course, at the Gildenhorn home, it is practically the opposite scene—the careless relinquishing of the Jewish religion in favor of the loutish habits and rituals of contemporary culture.

13. One could say that Mottshi Shaynbart and his ilk represent the exact opposite sentiment to the psalm. Instead of rejecting the culture around them for the sake of "Jerusalem," they indulge in the epicurean excesses of their surroundings, and completely forget their holy origins.

14. The narrator also lets the reader know that Gedalia is no paragon of selfless virtue. Even though Gedalia is known for his generous philanthropy, the narrator tells us that if it had not been for the thoughtfulness of Gedalia's wife Bertha, his own relatives would have gone hungry, for he never thought about them unless they showed up at his door (91 [3:138]).

15. Note that in the case of Tsirl, religion is perceived in a similarly superstitious light. Her desire for Hirshl to become a rabbi, for example, stems only from the primitive belief that in doing so her family might avoid the supposed curse that had been inflicted upon her great-great grandfather and his descendants (16 [3:66]).

16. One could speculate that this was more a prophecy than a curse. The fact that Tsirl's great-great grandfather was critical of "excessive" piety may show the incursion of modern ideas already within that family. Perhaps the rabbi rightly saw that with this type of impiety tainting religious life, there will be little religious life left to preserve in a few generations.

17. When Hirshl goes mad in the forest, Tsirl again thinks that it is because of the family curse. Rather than looking at the present reality of Hirshl's situation (i.e., Hirshl's unhappy marriage, etc., and her own role in his psychological imbalance), she prefers to rely on superstition to account for the purely human and avoidable pitfalls in life (See especially 179 [3:223]).

18. The question of whether Hirshl is a symbolic "everyman" (or "every Jewish man") is discussed in the final chapter (chapter 6) of this work.

19. Gedalia's willingness to passively accept whatever misfortune befalls him is well illustrated later in the novel when his son-in-law Hirshl is found babbling in the forest and declared mad. The narrator describes Gedalia's reaction to this tragedy befalling his family: "Gedalia alone took it calmly. All his life he had been waiting for disaster to strike, and now that it had he was not at all surprised" (174 [3:218]).

20. Clearly Mina is the allegorical equivalent to the straw bride in the tale. One can also see that the gold ring for which the man reaches has its allegorical parallel in Hirshl's desire for material comfort, a desire that has ultimately led to his unhappy marriage and a dull existence. Note that in Robert Alter's brief but penetrating interpretation of this mythic tale, he says that "the moment the man in the story succumbs to the temptation of gold, he irrevocably loses his soul." See Robert Alter, "Agnon's Psychological Realism," in *Hebrew and Modernity* (Bloomington: University of Indiana Press, 1994), 134-53, especially 148.

21. Hirshl is obviously aware of ideas of free will as derived from the biblical stories, but he does not think of *acting* according to their example. For instance, after Hirshl marries Mina, he begins to realize how unhappy he is. At one point, he compares his own fate to that of two biblical prototypes, Jacob and Elkanah, both of whom were bound to women they did not love and had to wait before they could find happiness with their true beloved ones. But Hirshl resigns himself to his fate with Mina, asking: "what was a man to do who could not give his beloved anything, having already given all away to the woman he hated?" (156 [3:201]).

22. Although Hillel Halkin translates the Hebrew word *letz* as "troll," its usual meaning is "clown," "mocker," or even "demon." In his English translation of the novel, Halkin likely chose "troll" to capture the mythic quality of the tale, and to impart the *sinister* aspect of these laughing creatures who trap the unwitting groom into laughing along with them. (Perhaps one should also note that a troll is a creature from Teutonic folklore who traps or baits; as a verb, "to troll" means "to fish" or "hook bait.")

23. It is surely significant that graves keep turning up in Szybusz whenever stones are turned, perhaps suggesting on a symbolic level that Jewish life of the past cannot be so easily forgotten, or "paved over." It is also significant that the historical scholar Akavia Mazal wrote a whole book about these graves beneath the town, Mazal being the only one in the novel who takes the past seriously (94 [3:141]).

24. In the case of Hirshl Hurvitz, here is a young Jew who knows much about the facts of local Jewish history, but yet generally does not want to think about it. For example, Hirshl tells Mina about the history of the town of Stanislaw (75-6 [3:123-4]), and of the cruelty of the town bailiff toward the Jews.

Mina finds it fascinating but cannot relate it at all to her present life, i.e., the past has little bearing on the present consciousness of the ordinary Jew. Persecution is a thing of the past for Mina, as it is for most Jews, including Hirshl, who possesses the factual knowledge but refuses to think through its possible implications in the present.

25. The idea that true freedom is connected to the understanding of one's past might be viewed as a "Freudian" insight that by implication Agnon seems to apply to historical memory as much as to childhood memory.

26. Considering this novel was published in 1935, it is more than likely that Agnon was highly aware of the dangers beginning to engulf the Jews of Europe. Although *Sipur pashut* is written about an earlier and more benign period (the turn of the twentieth century), Agnon clearly exhibits an acute awareness of how the average *galut* Jew such as Hirshl tends to deny the bitter experiences of the past and is thereby left unprepared for the possibility that these same realities could resurface and threaten his own future.

27. The folk in Szybusz may think that they have made great strides toward achieving freedom (and Agnon gleefully satirizes these "accomplishments"), but the perceptive reader can see how pathetic these attempts truly are. In fact, the people of Szybusz are generally shown to be enslaved by their own prejudices and ignorance. For example, they have little awareness of historical scholarship even as a means of understanding their own past. The narrator lets this be known to the reader in the scene at the sanatorium where Hirshl is astounded by the beauty of the Hasidic tales recounted to him by Rabbi Zanvil. About this ignorance in regard to Hasidism, the narrator says: "and while scholarly books about Hasidism and collections of their legends that showed them in a better light were available, no one in Galicia even bothered to read them, for the Hasidim considered them sacrilegious, while their opponents imagined a Hasidic anthology to be simply a kind of Jewish joke book" (188 [3:232]).

28. Note how Hirshl senses the greater authenticity of Akavia Mazal's entire form of Judaism. For example, he imagines that Akavia Mazal must surely build a nice sukkah on the outskirts of town, as compared to the ones in Szybusz proper, which repel Hirshl (114 [3:160]).

29. Despite the social scorn surrounding the marriage of Tirza to Akavia Mazal (he was more than twice her age, etc.), the couple ignored convention and followed their hearts, something that Tirza's own mother did not have the courage to do, and which seemed to lead to a broken heart and her untimely death. See Agnon's story "Bi-dmi yameha" in *Kol sipurav shel Shmuel Yosef 'Agnon,* 3:5-54.

30. Gershon Shaked sees the story of Akavia and Tirza Mazal as showing, among other things, that when love does not succeed in one generation (i.e., the love between Akavia and Tirza's mother), it eventually is able to succeed in the next generation. Although I partly agree with him on this point, I think he goes too far in connecting this fact with the fate of Blume Nacht. Shaked interprets Blume's retreat to the Mazal home as providing a hint of a similarly happy fate for Blume or those like her in the next generation, almost as a sort of fulfillment of a mythic archetypal pattern. If this was Agnon's intention, I believe he would have given the reader more of a solid indication of what lies ahead for

Blume. As I see it, Blume's future is unknown and remains in a kind of "suspended animation," since the love story between herself and Hirshl never came to fruition. Another way of speculating on Blume's (and Hirshl's) eventual fate is presented by Nitza Ben-Dov, who views it "intertextually." She sees their "reappearance" in the characters of Manfred Herbst and the nurse Shira in Agnon's final (posthumously published) novel *Shira*. Although there are definite similarities in the personalities of the main characters in these two novels, I think that if Agnon wanted to continue the story of Hirshl and Blume in a later novel, he would have simply placed them in it and called them by their own names, as he often did with other characters in many of his works. See Gershon Shaked, *Panim aherot be-yitsirato shel Shai 'Agnon* (Tel Aviv: Hakibutz hameukhad, 1989), 67-9; Nitza Ben-Dov, *Ahavot lo me'usharot: tiskul eroti, omanut, u-mavet bi-yetsirat 'Agnon.* (Tel Aviv, Israel: 'Am 'Oved, 1997), 237-8.

31. Note that there is the odd other individual in Szybusz who is aware of the importance of the past. For example, there is Hayyim Yehoshua Bleiberg (209 [3:252]), who is considered by the townsfolk to be a "queer duck" for just this very reason. No one in the town can understand why he is incensed about the painting over of the historic murals in the old synagogue with gold and silver polka-dots, "like those in the buffet of the railway station" (209 [3:252]). The rest of the town consider this "updating" of their synagogue to be a major advance toward modernization!

32. Though the narrator (with typical ironic naivete), seems "perplexed" by Dr. Langsam, he nevertheless implies that the doctor indulges in a kind of conscious denial. As he puts it: "Though he had studied in famous universities, lived in great metropolises, and frequented celebrated theaters and opera houses, all these places might as well never have existed: nothing had remained in his memory, it seemed, but the little town he grew up in, with its merchants saying Psalms in the marketplace, its rabbi making bookmarks [*sic*] with his fingernails, and its students struggling to decipher them" (189 [3:232-3]).

33. Note how Hirshl is moved by the old doctor's "sweet gruff sadness" when he sings him songs of his childhood (190 [3:233]); he also describes the doctor as having a "suffering face" (191 [3:234]).

34. Agnon was surely aware of the influence that literature had on life. It was well known that Goethe's novel *The Sorrows of Young Werther* (1774) caused many a lovelorn youth to imitate its tragic example and commit suicide. Flaubert's *Madame Bovary* (1857) apparently had a similar effect, even though Flaubert likely wrote it as a critique of such characters.

35. See for example Hillel Barzel, "Mavo," in *Shmuel Yosef 'Agnon: Mivhar ma'amarim 'al yetsirato* (Tel Aviv, Israel: 'Am 'Oved, 1982), 56-58. Cf. also Nitza Ben-Dov who says: "It is a tribute to the genius of Dr. Langsam—who despite his unconventional methods, is a brilliant diagnostician and therapist." Nitza Ben-Dov, *Agnon's Art of Indirection* (Leiden, The Netherlands: E. J. Brill, 1993), 98.

36. See David Biale, *Eros and the Jews* (New York: Basic Books, 1992), 149-75.

37. The origin of the idea of external freedom and internal slavery, especially as applied to the "emancipated" Jew of the diaspora, may well hearken back to the thought of the Zionist thinker Ahad Ha-'Am (Asher Ginzberg), who elucidated this concept in a well-known essay entitled "Avdut betokh Herut" ("Slavery in Freedom"), first published in 1891. See *Kol Kitve Ahad ha-'Am* (Tel Aviv, Israel: Dvir, 1964), 64-69.

38. It is on this point that my interpretation of Agnon's approach to religion diverges decisively from that of Baruch Kurzweil. Although Kurzweil also sees the decline of religion in Agnon's work as tied to the problem of eros, Kurzweil links eros solely with artistic creativity. I agree that love (eros) and creativity are indeed bound up together in Agnon's work (especially in stories such as "Agunot"), but I would add that Agnon understands political freedom to be a necessary precondition for such creativity. Kurzweil shifts attention away from the political factor in Agnon, because he seems to believe that the ultimate solution to the problem of eros in Agnon is through a revitalized spiritual-religious life that would tap the wellsprings of art and creativity among the Jews. Kurzweil may be correct insofar as he goes—but he does not go far enough. In other words, his view is incomplete because he does not sufficiently take account of the *fundamental* condition that would allow for the freeing up of the creative impulse—erotic, artistic, and religious—among the Jews, that is, *political* freedom. See Baruch Kurzweil, "Ha-yesod ha-dati be-kitve 'Agnon" in *Masot 'al Sipure Shai 'Agnon* (Tel Aviv, Israel: Schocken, 1970), 328-52.

39. Note that almost fifty years after Agnon wrote *Sipur pashut,* the Israeli writer Aharon Appelfeld employed a similar ironic technique to that of Agnon, portraying self-deception in the face of impending doom. This is particularly evident in novels by Appelfeld such as *Tor Ha-pelaot* (1978), *Badenheim, 'Ir Nofesh* (1980), and *Ha-pisgah* (1982). Of course, Appelfeld's portraits of Jewish life in the 1930s sound a much more ominous note, since they depict Jewish civilization on the very edge of destruction from a post-Holocaust perspective. Nevertheless, there is an uncanny similarity in the techniques used by Agnon and Appelfeld, for they both use hindsight in order to hold up an ironic mirror to the past, thereby capturing the ways in which the Jews fool themselves about the security of their existence.

40. See Gershon Shaked, *S. Y. Agnon: A Revolutionary Traditionalist* (New York: New York University Press, 1989), 130-6, and especially 136. I am in agreement with Gershon Shaked about the ironic nature of the "happy ending" of *Sipur pashut.* Shaked, however, sees the focus of Agnon's critique being directed almost entirely against the bourgeois nature of *galut* society. Although a critique of the Galician Jewish *bourgeoisie* is undoubtedly an essential part of Agnon's satire, I view the novel not only in socioeconomic terms but also in political terms: as a critique of the entire notion of a fruitful Jewish future in the *galut,* regardless of whether that future is bourgeois or not bourgeois.

41. Esther Fuchs makes the apt point that despite the formation of Zionist and Socialist organizations in Szybusz, nothing ever changes for the Jews in the town. In her view, this is because instead of being transformed by these revolutionary ideas, the townsfolk take these ideas and merely trivialize them. See Fuchs, *Omanut ha-hitamemut,* 96.

42. An example of this attitude is exemplified by Boruch Meir's disdain for his brother Meshúlam's idea of becoming a farmer in Israel (200 [3:243]).

43. The American Yiddish poet Jacob Glatstein captures this phenomenon in a poem entitled "God of My Forefathers" ("Got fun meyne avos"), wherein he says: "Anyway, without our God/ we have a funny look/ When they shaved you off from us/ we walked around looking like boy-Jews/ cheap vaudevillians." See *The Selected Poems of Jacob Glatstein,* trans. and ed. Ruth Whitman (New York: October House, 1972), 100-1; *Dem Tatns Shotn* (New York: Farlag Matones, 1953), 119-21.

Chapter 6

Conclusion: A Portrait of the Artist As an Ironic Romantic—The "Impossibility" of the Jewish Love Story

If, as I have been arguing, the political lens is the one through which Agnon casts his portrait of Szybusz society, then the question remains as to *why* this perspective has been overlooked by most literary scholars who have written about *Sipur pashut*.[1] This may be because the political nature of Agnon's portrayal is at once obvious and unobvious. It is obvious in the sense that in his personal life Agnon was a partisan of a distinct political movement, i.e., Zionism, which led him to settle in Palestine and become one of the major participants in the creation of a newly independent Jewish national culture. It is unobvious because Agnon does not present Szybusz society, at least in this novel, in a particularly political light. He merely displays all the symptoms of an ailing diaspora society, and lets the reader ponder as to what the causes of the illness might be. And yet Agnon drops sufficient hints to let the reader know where to begin the search and, above all, how to find out where *he* as the author of this novel stands.

And this is where the unobvious now becomes obvious. This is because, despite appearances to the contrary, politics is ever present in Agnon's novel. But it is ever present in a causative way, rather than an "effective" one. In other words, it remains the exclusive possession of the author himself, who only allows it to emerge here and there, like a puppeteer who occasionally allows his hands to show. Hence, Agnon's political vision might shape the course of events that ensue in his novel, but he only lets the reader know this through ironic interjections which contradict the conventional mores of the characters who inhabit Szybusz society.

The political perspective that therefore begins to emerge from these ironic hints and clues is one that sees Szybusz society as being hopelessly doomed to a kind of debased existence. Indeed, Agnon shows us what happens to Jews in *galut,* who have become so accustomed to their powerless state that they have ceased longing for independence. This is made all the worse by the fact that the inhabitants have made a virtue out of the perversities of their condition, elevating their trivial accomplishments to a level far above their real value.[2] Even a young man such as Hirshl Hurvitz, who is at times intensely critical of everything around him, cannot improve the societal landscape, not because he does not desire to do so, but because he shows no signs of knowing how to even initiate change. Being a son of Szybusz, he is intrinsically weak, so despite the promise he might show as one who dimly recognizes his society's inherent problems, he is unable to act on his perceptions. Thus a kind of vicious circle is generated, and the society stays ever the same, bequeathing weakness even to those most likely to be strong—its youth.

It is this self-perpetuating political abnormality of Jewish life, with the enormous influence it could not help but exercise on the psychological, social, and religious aspects of Jewish life, that points to why modern Jewish literature (outside of Israel) is markedly different from other world literatures. Exacerbating this centuries-old problem of Jewish "powerlessness" is the fact that modern Jewish literature arose during the late nineteenth and early twentieth centuries mostly in countries that were, even at the best of times, barely tolerant of Jews, and at the worst of times, murderously hostile. Although political vulnerability was not the only defining feature of Jewish life during this period, it was an unavoidable precondition which cast all other concerns in a kind of refracted light.

This is not to say that there are no similarities between Jewish literature and the works that were being produced in other cultures.

On the contrary, they inhabit much common ground, especially in terms of stylistics and trends in literary expression. But the point remains the same: when the writers of other cultures produce stories about the problems of their society, although they might be emotionally alienated from that society it is nevertheless their *own* nation; hence these writers possess within their very artistic vision the intrinsic hope, if not always the freedom, to strive for permanent change within a culture sustained by an *existing* national-political life. But Jews, and especially Jewish writers, have rarely been able to entertain such a hope, for their literary efforts are complicated by the fact that no matter how much they might strive to improve their lot, they are always at the mercy of nations to which they do not totally belong. In other words, even "alienation" takes on a different slant, and carries with it distinctly political implications.

Is it any wonder then that Agnon portrays the likelihood of a simple love story emerging naturally from within this context as being almost beyond the realm of possibility? As we have shown, there are also distinct social, psychological, and religious factors which are key to understanding the dynamics of failed love in Agnon's fictional portrayal. But if these were the *only* factors causing the problem, then surely modern innovations such as social activism, psychoanalysis, and religious reform would change things for the better, and transform a town like Szybusz into a place where life could be lived happily, and love could flourish. However, Agnon holds out no such hope in his novel. In fact, Agnon points to the futility of employing such "modern" adaptations to solve the problems of Jewish society—the quackery of Dr. Langsam's brand of "psychology" is a good case in point. Indeed, the tragic ending of the novel testifies to how such innovations do nothing to relieve the stagnation of the society, except fool the inhabitants into thinking that they are keeping up with the times. The utter gloominess of the ending (made all the more searing by the pretense of Hirshl's new-found "happiness") is Agnon's way of saying that nothing has changed in Szybusz and nothing ever will. Such a thoroughly damning, if ironic, critique could only come from a political judgment that a healthy Jewish future in places like Szybusz is not to be expected. That is to say, if Jewish love stories

are to become a possibility, they will not take place within that
society, but only outside of it.

Does this therefore imply that Agnon's perspective is essentially a "Zionist" one? Although it is tempting to make that leap, it
could be hazardous to do so, for it might limit the scope of
Agnon's vision by wrongly subsuming all his work under the rubric
of Zionist ideology. Also, it is clear that Agnon was first and fore-
most a literary artist who, for the sake of his creative muse, jeal-
ously guarded his artistic independence from the crude mouthing of
slogans or the mere proclaiming of an ideology. At the same time, it
would be a disservice to the writer to assume that he holds no fixed
views, and it would be an injustice not to consider whether he
might not also be a thinker, as if a true artiste by definition is so far
removed from the world of political opinion that he could not possibly subscribe to any practical ideology.

The answer I would proffer to the above leading question is a
qualified "yes," since only in the broadest definition of the term
would it be fitting to call this novel a "Zionist work." On the one
hand, Agnon's portrait of Szybusz is undoubtedly a kind of fictional embodiment of the type of *galut* society of which the earlier
writers attached to Zionism were so critical (e.g., Berdyczewski
and Bialik). On the other hand, nowhere in the novel is there any
clear suggestion of a Zionist vision that could or even should be ac-
tualized, except for a few oblique references that are covered in
several layers of irony.[3] It may be more appropriate merely to say
that this is an ironic portrait of *galut* Jews written in the spirit of
Zionist criticism, but presented in a way that allows the reader to
draw the logical conclusions from it. Certainly those conclusions
would seem to point with the utmost suggestiveness in the
direction of a return to Jewish nationhood in Palestine as the only
way out of the beleaguered existence that is symbolized by the vicious circularity of Hirshl Hurvitz's story. This, however, is something that Agnon with his typical "art of indirection"[4] prefers
never to say outright. Instead, those conclusions are left to be
drawn more from what he does *not* say, allowing the underlying
logic of his narrative to point unfailingly to them. In this way,
Agnon trusts the narrative itself to open the eyes of thoughtful

readers, letting them grasp the political perspective which guided him, but which he, as an artist, preferred to leave undeclared.

Nevertheless, from the specificity of this political-artistic vantage point, it becomes evident that Agnon has created a kind of Jewish "everyman" in the figure of Hirshl Hurvitz, who transcends time and place and who represents a generic failing, even an essential flaw, at the heart of modern Jewish diaspora life. Whether or not Agnon intended to create a Jewish prototype is not our concern, but it is nonetheless a curious thing that one may discover Hirshl-like figures (weak-willed, indecisive, malleable, and obsessive) popping up in modern Jewish literature written in various languages and cultural contexts in the seventy years since *Sipur pashut* was published, and long after towns like Szybusz have ceased to exist. (One need look no further than Philip Roth's works to witness such recurrent "sightings" of the Hirshl-type.)[5] This is not to suggest that other writers have necessarily been influenced by Agnon, for it is doubtful whether the majority of these disparate writers would have even read Agnon's work. It merely proves how Agnon seems to have captured an essential *truth* about Jewish existence outside of Israel by creating a character-type that, like it or not, seems to persistently reappear, mutatis mutandis, in a variety of modern Jewish literary formats and cultural milieus.[6]

On a final note that is more speculative in nature, I would like to momentarily step outside the modest role of literary interpreter, and consider the possible biographical source of the Hirshl prototype, which may shed further light on the larger artistic vision in this novel. I would like to suggest that the figure of Hirshl Hurvitz is precisely what Shmuel Yosef Agnon dreaded he himself would have become if he had stayed in Buczacz and continued the life prescribed for him as Shmuel Yosef Czaczkes. In other words, Hirshl Hurvitz is a portrait of the artist as a young man, not as Agnon was in actuality, but as he *would have been* if he had stayed and lived out his youth in Galicia. (It is the "road not taken"[7]—and thankfully so!) Thus, the story of Hirshl and *Sipur pashut* could be seen as a sort of mirror held up to Agnon's own life as he might have lived it, with even the turn-of-the-century dating of the novel corresponding to the time of his own youth. Perhaps it is no coincidence that Hirshl is approximately the same age in the novel that Agnon himself would have been in that same time-frame.

But instead of living the kind of stultifying life that Hirshl did, Agnon followed his romantic aspirations and left Galicia to join the pioneers of the *yishuv* in Palestine, even though this meant leaving behind an ailing mother to whom he was strongly attached.[8] Although it is unclear whether the mature Agnon ultimately considered the rebirth of Jewish national life in Palestine to be a full realization of that youthful dream, this does not change the fact that he left Galicia never to live there again. No one can know with any certainty how Agnon felt about leaving the place of his childhood—whether he was filled with guilt, relief, or self-justification. By the time of his writing *Sipur pashut* (the early 1930s), he was certainly aware of the mounting anti-Jewish ferment in eastern Europe stimulated by the rise of Nazism in Germany. This is the historical-political context out of which *Sipur pashut* was born, even though the reader would be hard pressed to find any direct evidence of it in the novel. Nevertheless, it is important to make note of it, even if only to ponder why Agnon seemingly makes so *little* of it.

If the technique that Agnon used in writing this novel is one that tries to conceal the present while looking back at the past, this could be seen as an attempt to understand the past (i.e., *his* past) on its own terms. Certainly the ominous fate that was threatening Galician Jewry in the present in which he was writing the novel may have suggested to him that something was wrong in its past that things had been allowed to come to such a desperate impasse. Was it utterly impossible to see such a situation of existing vulnerability and potential danger? If it were possible, what would a society look like which is so prone to self-deception? Were there no indications that Galician Jewish society (if not modern diaspora Jewry) was so "unhealthy" that it could not even detect its own symptoms?

In trying to understand the past on its own terms, it is plausible that Agnon set before himself a challenge: he would attempt to write a simple love story set in Szybusz, on the assumption that love serves as a kind of litmus test for a healthy and normal existence. Like a scientist performing his experiment, he would assemble the requisite materials and see whether his hypothesis is correct: that love stories cannot take root in such inhospitable soil. If his hypothesis is wrong, and love is still able to flourish in Szybusz, then perhaps the Jews cannot be blamed for placing their trust in towns like Szybusz. But if his hypothesis is proved correct in the novel, as by now we know it is, then he was right about the untenable nature of Jewish life in Szybusz. Hence, according to the controlled conditions of his own experiment as an author, the act of writing this novel may have proven to Agnon himself that he had been right to leave *his* Szybusz (i.e., Buczacz) as early as he did (in 1907)[9] before he was doomed to become Hirshl Hurvitz, or worse. In other words, the story of Hirshl Hurvitz is a potent reminder of what could have been Agnon's own tragic fate. And lest he ever doubt the wisdom of his departure from that world, *Sipur pashut* could be seen as a permanent testimony to the necessity of his own choice.

If this seems like a fanciful interpretation of Agnon's motives for creating a romantic love story and then turning it on its head, it becomes more plausible if one looks at it in light of Agnon as a *thinker* rather than merely as a writer who needed to "purge" his guilt. The question of the novel is not only about Hirshl (i.e., young Agnon *in potentia*), but also about the masses of Jews like Hirshl who stayed in places like Szybusz. Although the novel examines how it was that the people of Szybusz-Buczacz refused to see the false basis of their own existence, Agnon does not preach about it; he was too much of an artist to succumb to the temptation of letting his political position spoil his art. This is where the attempt at creating a romance transforms itself into an ironic version of the same. Instead of lamenting the fact of Hirshl's ineptitude, or bitterly chastising the people of Szybusz for their blindness, Agnon lets the story be narrated with ironic detachment, allowing his characters to speak for themselves.

As a novelist-thinker trying to understand his past in the broadest sense of the term, Agnon attempts in *Sipur pashut* to recreate that past world in a way that encourages the reader to decide for himself how to interpret its failings; in this sense, it is also a story about *human* failings with which any reader can identify. Self-deception and weakness of will are not the sole possessions of diaspora Jews. Likewise, failure to pursue a dream is what haunts most tragic heroes, not just Jewish ones. This is why the novel "works" even if the reader does not know when it was written and why. It stands on its own as a portrait of a young man beaten by the society he loathes.

But then again, it is also more. It is a story about love and its utter failure in a world devoid of romance. If Jewish life lacks romance, Agnon's portrait tells us why: romance needs heroes; heroes need courage; courage needs will; and will needs independence. It should not surprise us that Hirshl possesses none of these "building blocks," since his society cannot even provide the foundation stone: political independence. And this leads again to the problem of political life in Agnon's vision of love. If the lack of Jewish political independence tacitly spells the doom of love between Hirshl and Blume, and therefore the impossibility of the Jewish love story, then the message would seem to be clear: Jewish life will only be able to correct this abnormality by seeking a political overturning of its situation—be it by Zionism or by some other revolutionary means. Only then might Jews be able to imagine a hero who possesses the necessary independence, will, and courage to pursue his beloved, as well as his destiny, freely. And only then might there be created a Jewish society that is everything Szybusz is not. *Sipur pashut* may not be Agnon's last word on love, but it is his most complete statement, gathering together in one work much that Jewish writers in the diaspora before him seemed to sense, and all that those after him have tragically confirmed. Beyond the irony, Agnon's vision may be seen to imply a romantic hope for the future, perhaps more than he himself could artistically achieve—that by willing it, the Jewish love story might someday be more than just a dream.

Notes

1. One exception is Yehuda Friedlander, whose early article on Agnon ends by emphasizing the political "axis" on which most of Agnon's works turn (i.e., Zionism). See Yehuda Friedlander, "ha-klal ve-ha-prat be-sipure 'Agnon," in *Yuval Shai likvod Shai 'Agnon,* ed. Baruch Kurzweil (Ramat Gan, Israel: Bar-Ilan University, 1958), 61-77, and especially 75-7. See also Gershom Scholem, "S. Y. Agnon—The Last Hebrew Classic?" in *On Jews and Judaism in Crisis,* ed. Werner J. Dannhauser (New York: Schocken, 1976), 93-116.

2. There are numerous examples of this throughout the novel, some of which are juxtaposed with events that would normally be endowed with respect, thereby adding to the irony by means of contrast. For example, more detailed attention is given to the exotic foods and foreign cigarettes offered at the engagement dinner of Hirshl and Mina, than is given to the bride and groom (77-83 [3:125-31]).

3. For instance, the discussion between Hirshl and Yona Toyber about their views of Zionism shows that although they both agree that the Jews should give up "buying and selling" and must return to "tilling the land," this has no bearing on their personal lives nor does it lead them to any political conclusions. In fact, Toyber then goes on to praise Gedalia Ziemlich because he lives on a farm, implying that Ziemlich is somehow participating in the Zionist project, which the reader of course knows is a farfetched, if not an absurd, suggestion. This is because (as the reader has just learned) Gedalia Ziemlich is an estate manager for the local Count, thus living on the land only on the good graces of his gentile overlord (95 [3:142]).

4. See Nitza Ben-Dov, *Agnon's Art of Indirection* (Leiden, The Netherlands: E. J. Brill, 1993).

5. One could go so far as to say that Philip Roth's Alexander Portnoy of *Portnoy's Complaint* (1969) is a sort of cruder, Americanized version of Hirshl Hurvitz. Other examples of works in which Hirshl-like characters appear are Bernard Malamud's *A New Life* (1961) and Bruce Jay Friedman's *Stern* (1962). One might also include here Saul Bellow's *Dangling Man* (1944) and *Herzog* (1964), although with the important qualification that Bellow's heroes tend to transcend their passive state by the end of the novels.

6. In some ways the Hirshl-type could be seen as merely a variation on the *schlemiel,* a character type who originates in Jewish folklore and who often reappears in much of modern Jewish literature. However, one important qualification is in order. As Ruth Wisse has persuasively argued, the *schlemiel* character (at least within Yiddish literature) possesses a kind of "heroism," for in contradistinction to the brutality of the world around him, he maintains a type of inner nobility, in spite of his outer comic persona. I would contend that whereas "heroism" is certainly applicable to the *schlemiel* of Yiddish literature, it is not necessarily the case with Hebrew literature, in which the *schlemiel* is generally depicted in a much more negative light. Indeed, the difference between the *schlemiel* in the two literatures might underscore a fundamental difference in sensibility between the two camps. In this regard, Agnon undoubtedly falls into

the Hebrew camp, for although Hirshl might be a *schlemiel,* he is certainly no hero! See Ruth R. Wisse, *The Schlemiel As Modern Hero* (Chicago: University of Chicago Press, 1971).

7. See the well-known poem by Robert Frost, "The Road Not Taken," in *Mountain Interval* (New York: Holt, 1916).

8. See Arnold Band, *Nostalgia and Nightmare* (Berkeley: University of California Press, 1968), 1-28, and especially 8.

9. Although there is some confusion as to the actual year that Agnon left Buczacz, the careful research of Arnold Band shows that it was in 1907 (rather than in 1908 or 1909, as had previously been documented). Since Agnon's mother died in 1908, his leaving must have generated considerable guilt on his part, and perhaps a desire to justify his decision in later years. See Band, *Nostalgia and Nightmare*, 16, note 20.

Bibliography

Aberbach, David. *At the Handles of the Lock.* New York: Oxford University Press, 1984.

———. "Fantasies of Deviance in Mendele and Agnon," *AJS Review* 19/1 (1994): 45-60.

Abramowitz, Shalom (Mendele Mocher Seforim). *Fishke der krumer.* 2nd ed. In *Ale verk fun Mendele Moykher Sforim.* vol 1. Odessa, Russia: Varshaver, 1888.

———. *Fishke the Lame,* trans. Gerald Stillman. New York: Thomas Yoseloff, 1960.

Abrams, M. H. "How to Do Things with Texts." *Partisan Review* 46 (1979): 566-88.

———. *The Mirror and the Lamp: Romantic Theory and the Critical Tradition.* New York: Oxford University Press, 1953.

Agnon, Shmuel Yosef. *A Book That Was Lost, and Other Stories,* ed. Alan Mintz and Anne Golomb Hoffman. New York: Schocken, 1995.

———. *The Bridal Canopy,* trans. I. M. Lask. New York: Schocken, 1967.

———. *A Guest for the Night,* trans. Misha Louvish. New York: Schocken, 1968.

———. *Kol sipurav shel Shmuel Yosef 'Agnon,* 1st ed. vol. 5. Berlin: Schocken, 1935.

———. *Kol sipurav shel Shmuel Yosef 'Agnon.,* 2nd ed. 8 vols. Tel Aviv, Israel: Schocken, 1953-62.

———. *Only Yesterday,* trans. Barbara Harshav. Princeton, N.J.: Princeton University Press, 2000.

———. *A Poshete Ma'ase,* trans. Eliezer Rubinstein. New York: Der Kval, 1958.

———. *Shira,* ed. Emuna Yaron. Tel Aviv, Israel: Schocken, 1971.

———. *Shira,* trans. Zeva Shapiro. New York: Schocken, 1989.

———. *Sh. Y. 'Agnon—Sh. Z. Shoken: hilufe igrot.* Jerusalem: Schocken, 1991.

———. *A Simple Story,* trans. Hillel Halkin. New York: Schocken, 1985.

———. *Twenty-One Stories,* ed. and trans. Nahum N. Glatzer. New York: Schocken, 1970.

———. *Two Tales: Betrothed, and Edo and Enam,* trans. Walter Lever. New York: Schocken, 1966.

Alter, Robert. *After the Tradition.* New York: Dutton, 1969.

———. *The Art of Biblical Narrative.* New York: Basic Books, 1981.

———. *Defenses of the Imagination*. Philadelphia: Jewish Publication Society, 1977.

———. *Hebrew and Modernity*. Bloomington,: Indiana University Press, 1994.

———. *The Invention of Hebrew Prose*. Seattle: University of Washington Press, 1988.

———. *The Pleasures of Reading in an Ideological Age*. New York: Simon and Schuster, 1989.

Anski, S. *The Dybbuk and Other Writings*, ed. David Roskies, and trans. Golda Werman. New York: Schocken, 1992.

———. "Der Dybuk." 7-105 in *Gezamelte Schriften*, vol. 2. Warsaw, Poland: An-Ski, 1925.

Artz, Frederick. *From the Renaissance to Romanticism*. Chicago: University of Chicago Press, 1962.

Babbitt, Irving. *Rousseau and Romanticism*. Austin: University of Texas Press, 1977.

Bakhtin, Mikhail. *The Dialogic Imagination: Four Essays*, ed. M. Holquist, and trans. M. Holquist and C. Emerson. Austin: University of Texas Press, 1987.

Band, Arnold. *Nostalgia and Nightmare*. Berkeley: University of California Press, 1968.

Bar-El, Joseph. "Tshatshkis, Agnon, and the Etymology of Shibesh." *Oksforder Yidish: A Yearbook of Yiddish Studies* 2 (1991): 3-16.

Bargad, Warren. "Agnon and German Neoromanticism." *Prooftexts* 1 (1981): 96-8.

Barzel, Hillel. *Beyn Agnon le-Kafka: Mehkar mashveh*. Ramat Gan, Israel: Bar-Ilan University Press, 1972.

———."Mavo." 9-168 in *Shmuel Yosef 'Agnon: Mivhar ma'amarim 'al yetsirato*, ed. Hillel Barzel. Tel Aviv, Israel: 'Am 'Oved, 1982.

———. "ha-Roved ha-agadi be-sipurei Ahava shel Shai 'Agnon." *Gazit* 30/5-8 (1963-64): 8-11.

———. "Sh. Y. 'Agnon—gilui ve-ne'elam." 131-75 in *Hikre 'Agnon: 'Iyyunim le-Professor Yehuda Friedlander*, eds. Hillel Weiss and Hillel Barzel. Ramat Gan, Israel: Bar-Ilan University Press, 1994.

———, ed. *Sippurei ahavah shel Shmuel Yosef 'Agnon: 'Iyyunei Mehkar*. Ramat Gan, Israel: Bar-Ilan University Press, 1975.

Barzun, Jacques. *Classic, Romantic, and Modern*. New York: Anchor, 1961.

———. *Darwin, Marx, Wagner*. New York: Doubleday Anchor, 1958.

———. *Romanticism and the Modern Ego*. Boston: Little, Brown, 1943.

Bate, Walter Jackson. *From Classic to Romantic*. Cambridge, Mass.: Harvard University Press, 1949.

Bellow, Saul. "Introduction." 9-16 in *Great Jewish Short Stories*, ed. Saul Bellow. New York: Dell, 1963.

Ben-Dov, Nitza. *Agnon's Art of Indirection*. Leiden, The Netherlands: E. J. Brill, 1993.

———. *Ahavot lo me'usharot: tiskul eroti, omanut, u-mavet bi-yetsirat 'Agnon*. Tel Aviv, Israel: 'Am 'Oved, 1997.

———. "Discriminated Occasion and Discrete Conflicts in Agnon's *A Simple Story*." *Prooftexts* 9 (1989): 213-28.

Benjamin, Walter. *Illuminations*. Ed. Hannah Arendt, and trans.Harry Zohn. New York: Schocken, 1968.

Biale, David. *Eros and the Jews*. New York: Basic Books, 1992.

Bloom, Allan. *Love and Friendship*. New York: Simon and Schuster, 1993.

Bloom, Harold, ed. *D. H. Lawrence*. New York: Chelsea House, 1986.

———. ed. *Franz Kafka*. New York: Chelsea House, 1986.

———. *Romanticism and Consciousness*. New York: Norton, 1970.

Boone, Joseph Allen. *Tradition Counter Tradition: Love and the Form of Fiction*. Chicago: University of Chicago Press, 1987.

Booth, Wayne, *The Rhetoric of Fiction*. Chicago: University of Chicago Press, 1961.

Brandwein, Naftali. "S. Y. Agnon: Alienation and Return." *Jewish Book Annual* 25 (1967-8): 27-38.

Brombert, Victor, ed. *The Hero in Literature*. Greenwich, Conn.: Fawcett, 1969.

Coffin, Edna Amir. "Do Words Conceal or Reveal Intent of Verbal Expressions? Thought Process and Written Symbols in Agnon's Fiction." In *Agnon: Texts and Contexts in English Translation*, ed. Leon I. Yudkin. New York: Markus Wiener, 1988.

Copleston, Frederick. *Friedrich Nietzsche: Philosopher of Culture*. London: Burns, Oates, and Washbourne, 1942.

Cutter, William. "Figurative Language in Agnon's *Sipur pashut*." *Prooftexts* 1 (1981): 311-15.

———. "Rendering Galicia for America: On Hillel Halkin's Translation of *Sipur pashut*." *Prooftexts* 7 (1987): 73-88.

———. "Setting As a Feature of Ambiguity in S. Y. Agnon's *Sipur pashut*." *Critique* 15/3 (1974): 66-80.

Davies, Robertson. *The Mirror of Nature*. Toronto: University of Toronto Press, 1983.

De Rougemont, Denis. *Love in the Western World*. Princeton, N.J.: Princeton University Press, 1983.

Dundes, Alan, ed. *Cinderella: A Folklore Casebook*. New York: Garland, 1982.

Epstein, Joseph. "Our Debt to I. B. Singer." *Commentary* 92/5 (November 1991): 31-7.

Ewen, Josef. "He'arot ahadot le-*Sipur pashut* le-Shai 'Agnon." *Moznayim* 29 (1970): 400-414.

Fisch, Harold. *S. Y. Agnon*. New York: Frederick Ungar, 1975.

Forster, E. M. *Aspects of the Novel*. New York: Harcourt Brace Jovanovich, 1954.

Freud, Sigmund. *A General Introduction to Psychoanalysis*. New York: Washington Square Press, 1924.

Friedlander, Yehuda. "ha-Klal ve-ha-prat be-sipure 'Agnon." 61-77 in *Yuval Shai likvod Shai 'Agnon*, ed. Baruch Kurzweil. Ramat Gan, Israel: Bar-Ilan University, 1958.

Frye, Northrop. *Anatomy of Criticism*. Princeton, N.J.: Princeton University Press, 1957.

———. *The Critical Path: An Essay on the Social Context of Literary Criticism*. Bloomington: Indiana University Press, 1971.

———. *A Natural Perspective*. New York: Columbia University Press, 1965.

————. *The Secular Scripture*. Cambridge, Mass.: Harvard University Press, 1976.

Fuchs, Esther. "Ironiç Characterization in the Works of S. Y. Agnon." *AJS Review* 7-8 (1982-83): 101-28.

————. *Omanut ha-hitamemut: 'al ha-'ironiah shel Shai 'Agnon*. Tel Aviv, Israel: Tel Aviv University Press, 1985.

————. *Sehoq samui: Heibetim qomiyim ba-yitsirah ha-'agnonit*. Tel Aviv, Israel: Tel Aviv University Press, 1987.

Gay, Peter. *The Bourgeois Experience*. Oxford: Oxford University Press, 1986.

Ginzberg, Asher (Ahad Ha-'Am). "Avdut betokh Herut." 64-9 in *Kol Kitve Ahad ha'Am*. Tel Aviv, Israel: Dvir, 1964.

Glatstein, Jacob. *Dem Tatns Shotn*. New York: Farlag Matones, 1953.

————. *The Selected Poems of Jacob Glatstein*, trans. and ed. Ruth Whitman. New York: October House, 1972.

Glicksberg, Charles I. *Literature and Society*. The Hague: Martinus Nijhoff, 1972.

Graff, Gerald. *Literature Against Itself*. Chicago: University of Chicago Press, 1979.

Hagstrum, Jean H. *Sex and Sensibility: Ideal and Erotic Love from Milton to Mozart*. Chicago: University of Chicago Press, 1980.

Hakak, Lev. "Motif ha-tarnigol be-*Sipur pashut* le-Shai 'Agnon." *Hasifrut* 4/4 (1973): 713-25.

Halkin, Hillel. "Afterword." 231-46 in *A Simple Story*, trans. Hillel Halkin. New York: Schocken, 1985.

Halkin, Simon. *Modern Hebrew Literature: Trends and Values*. New York: Schocken, 1970.

Heller, Erich. *The Artist's Journey Into the Interior, and Other Essays*. New York: Random House, 1965.

Hirsch, E. D. *Validity in Interpretation*. New Haven, Conn.: Yale University Press, 1967.

Hochman, Baruch. *The Fiction of S. Y. Agnon*. Ithaca, N.Y.: Cornell University Press, 1970.

Hoffman, Anne Golomb. "Agnon for All Seasons: Recent Trends in the Criticism." *Prooftexts* 11 (1991): 81-96.

————. *Between Exile and Return: S. Y. Agnon and the Drama of Writing*. Albany: State University of New York Press, 1991.

Hoffman, Frederick. *Freudianism and the Literary Mind*. Baton Rouge: Louisiana State University Press, 1975.

Howe, Irving. *The Critical Point: On Literature and Culture*. New York: Dell, 1973.

————. *Politics and the Novel*. New York: Meridian, 1987.

————. *Selected Writings 1950-1990*. New York: Harcourt Brace Jovanovich, 1990.

Hunt, Morton M. *The Natural History of Love*. New York: Alfred A. Knopf, 1959.

Josipovici, Gabriel, ed. *The Modern English Novel*. London: Open Books, 1976.

Katz, Jacob. *Out of the Ghetto: The Social Background of Jewish Emancipation 1770-1870*. New York: Schocken, 1978.

———. *Tradition and Crisis: Jewish Society at the End of the Middle Ages.* New York: Schocken, 1961.

Katz, Stephen. *The Centrifugal Novel: S. Y. Agnon's Poetics of Composition.* Madison, N.J.: Farleigh Dickenson University Press, 1999.

Kermode, Frank. *The Sense of an Ending: Studies in the Theory of Fiction.* New York: Oxford University Press, 1967.

Kernan, Alvin. *The Death of Literature.* New Haven, Conn.: Yale University Press, 1990.

Koestler, Arthur, ed. *The God That Failed.* London: Hamish Hamilton, 1950.

Krich, Aron M., ed. *The Anatomy of Love: A Collection of Essays.* New York: Dell, 1960.

Kurzweil, Baruch. *Masot 'al sipure Shai 'Agnon.* Jerusalem: Schocken, 1970.

———. "Religion in Agnon's Work." *Ariel* 17 (winter 1966-67): 7-30.

Lachower, Fischel. *Toledot ha-sifrut ha-ivrit ha-hadasha.* Tel Aviv, Israel: Dvir, 1948.

Landau, Dov. *Mi-signon le-mashma'ut be-sipure Shai 'Agnon.* Tel Aviv, Israel: Eked, 1988.

Levin, Harry. *Refractions: Essays in Comparative Literature.* New York: Oxford University Press, 1966.

Lodge, David. *After Bakhtin: Essays on Fiction and Criticism.* London: Routledge, 1990.

Mazor, Yair. *The Triple Cord: Agnon, Hamsun, and Strindberg.* Tel Aviv, Israel: Tel Aviv University Press, 1987.

Memmi, Albert. *The Liberation of the Jew.* New York: Viking, 1973.

———. *The Portrait of a Jew.* New York: Orion, 1962.

Mintz, Alan. "Agnon in Jaffa: The Myth of the Artist As a Young Man." *Prooftexts* 1 (1980): 62-83.

Miron, Dan. "Domesticating a Foreign Genre: Agnon's Transactions with the Novel," trans. Naomi B. Sokoloff. *Prooftexts* 7 (1987): 1-27.

———. "German Jews in Agnon's Work." *Leo Baeck Institute Yearbook* 23 (1978): 265-80.

———. *A Traveller Disguised.* New York: Schocken, 1973.

Niger, S. *Dertzeyler un Romanisten.* New York: 'Cyco' Bicher-Farlag, 1946.

Opie, Iona, and Peter Opie. *The Classic Fairy Tales.* London: Oxford University Press, 1974.

Oz, Amos. *Shtikat Ha-shamayim: Agnon Mishtomem 'Al Elohim.* Jerusalem: Keter, 1993.

———. *The Silence of Heaven: Agnon's Fear of God,* trans. Barbara Harshav. Princeton, N.J.: Princeton University Press, 2000.

Ozick, Cynthia. "S. Y. Agnon and the First Religion." 209-22 in *Metaphor and Memory: Essays.* New York: Alfred A. Knopf, 1989.

Patterson, David, and Abramson, Glenda, eds. *Tradition and Trauma: Studies in the Fiction of S. J. Agnon.* Boulder, Colo.: Westview Press, 1994.

Priestley, J. B. *Literature and Western Man.* New York: Harper and Row, 1960.

Rabinowicz, Tzvi, ed. *The Prince Who Turned into a Rooster.* Northvale, N.J.: Jason Aronson, 1993.

Rabinowitz, Sholom (Sholom Aleichem). *The Best of Sholom Aleichem,* ed. Irving Howe and Ruth R. Wisse. New York: Simon and Schuster, 1979.

————. *Shomer's Mishpet.* Berdichev, Russia: Spector, 1888.

Rahill, Frank. *The World of Melodrama.* University Park: Pennsylvania State University Press, 1967.

Rousseau, Jean-Jacques. *Emile, or On Education,* trans. Allan Bloom. New York: Basic Books, 1979.

Sadan, Dov, and Urbach, E. E., eds. *le-'Agnon Shai: Devarim 'al ha-Sofer ve-Sipurav.* Jerusalem: Jewish Agency, 1959.

————. "Sipur 'al *Sipur pashut.*" 36-40 in *'Al Shmuel Yosef 'Agnon.* Tel Aviv, Israel: Hakibbutz Hameuchad, 1973.

Scholem, Gershom. "S. Y. Agnon—The Last Hebrew Classic?" 93-116 in *On Jews and Judaism in Crisis,* ed. Werner J. Dannhauser. New York: Schocken, 1976.

Scholes, Robert, and Robert Kellogg. *The Nature of Narrative.* London: Oxford University Press, 1966.

Shaked, Gershon. "Bat ha-melekh ve-se'udat ha-em." 259-92 in *Shai 'Agnon: mivhar ma'amarim 'al yetzirato,* ed. Hillel Barzel. Tel Aviv, Israel: Tel Aviv University Press, 1982.

————. "Hayyim ba-Nes—Sh. Y. 'Agnon: Dramot ha-hevratiot ve-mimushan ha-sifruti." *Iton* 77/9 (July-August 1985): 22-4.

————. *'Omanut ha-sipur shel 'Agnon.* Tel Aviv, Israel: Sifri'at Poalim, 1973.

————. *Panim aherot be-yetsirato shel Shai 'Agnon.* Tel Aviv, Israel: Hakibbutz Hameuchad, 1989.

————. "Portrait of the Immigrant as a Young Neurotic." *Prooftexts* 7 (1987): 41-52.

————. *The Shadows Within: Essays on Modern Jewish Writers.* Philadelphia: Jewish Publication Society, 1987.

————. *Shmuel Yosef Agnon: A Revolutionary Traditionalist,* trans. Jeffrey Green. New York: New York University Press, 1989.

————. *Ha-Siporet ha-'ivrit 1880-1980,* in two volumes. Volume 1, Jerusalem, Israel: Keter, 1983; Volume 2, Tel Aviv, Israel: Hakibbutz Hameuchad, 1988.

Shaked, Malka. "Ha-im haya Hirshl meshug'a? Likrat ra'ya pluralistit shel ha-'alilah be-*Sipur pashut.*" *Hasifrut* 32 (June 1982): 132-47.

Shreibaum, Dvora. *Pesher ha-halomot bi-yetsirotav shel Sh. Y. 'Agnon.* Tel Aviv, Israel: Papyrus, 1993.

Singer, Irving. *The Nature of Love* (in three volumes). Chicago: University of Chicago Press, 1987.

Stern, Dina. "Ba'ayot ha-talut ve-hizdahut be-haye Hirshl Hurvitz: iyyun sifruti-psychologi be-*Sipur pashut* le-Shai 'Agnon." *Bi-Sadeh Hemed* 13 (1971): 296-303.

Tochner, Meshulam. *Pesher Agnon.* Tel Aviv, Israel: Masada, 1968.

Treatise Ta'anit of the Babylonian Talmud, ed. and trans. Henry Malter. Philadelphia: Jewish Publication Society, 1978.

Trilling, Lionel. *The Liberal Imagination.* New York: Doubleday Anchor, 1954.

————. *The Opposing Self: Nine Essays in Criticism.* New York: Harcourt Brace Jovanovich, 1978.

Udoff, Alan, ed. *Kafka and the Contemporary Critical Performance.* Bloomington: Indiana University Press, 1987.

Watt, Ian. *The Rise of the Novel*. Berkeley: University of California Press, 1957.

Wellek, Rene. *The Attack on Literature, and Other Essays*. Chapel Hill: University of North Carolina Press, 1982.

———. *Concepts of Criticism*. New Haven, Conn.: Yale University Press, 1963.

Wellek, Rene, and Austin Warren. *Theory of Literature*. New York: Harcourt Brace, 1956.

Werses, Shmuel. *Shai 'Agnon ki-feshuto: keri'ah bi-khetavav*. Jerusalem: Mosad Bialik, 2000.

Wirth-Nesher, Hana, ed. *What Is Jewish Literature?* Philadelphia: Jewish Publication Society, 1994.

Wisse, Ruth R. *The Schlemiel As Modern Hero*. Chicago: University of Chicago Press, 1971.

Yehoshua, A.B. "Plot and Denouement in *Sipur pashut*." 137-61 in *Agnon: Texts and Contexts in English Translation*, ed. Leon I. Yudkin. New York: Markus Wiener, 1988.

Yudkin, Leon I. *Jewish Writing and Identity in the Twentieth Century*. London: Croom Helm, 1982.

Index

Aberbach, David, 75n2, 75n5,
106n18, 109n35, 112n51
Abramowitz, Shalom Yacov
(pseud. Mendele Mocher
Sforim), 21, 23-24, 34n46-7,
34n52, 34n58, 44, 56n11,
77n21, 109n34
Abrams, M. H., 32n34, 33n42
Aesop, 108n29
Agnon, Shmuel Yosef (Shmuel
Yosef Czaczkes): biography,
139, 143-45, 148n8-9; critique
of Jewish society in work of,
26, 27, 35, 46, 51, 55n1,
57n24, 114, 129, 134n27,
136n40, 141, 142, 144, 146; as
Hebrew modernist, 2, 4, 26,
27; literary techniques, ix, 2,
4, 26, 34n57, 36, 77n19, 99,
101, 111n45, 111n48, 114,
125, 129, 131n5, 136n39, 139,
140, 142, 144-45, 147n2,
147n4; love stories of, 1,
29n10, 141; Nobel Prize
winner, ix; as thinker, ix, x,
132n10, 136n38, 139, 142,
145; works: "Agunot,"
136n38; "Bi-dmi yameha" ("In
the Prime of her Life"), 28n2,
57n26, 134-35nn29-30; "Bi-
n'arenu u-vi-zkenenu" ("With
Our Youth and With Our
Aged"), 55n5; "Ha-rofe u-
gerushato" ("The Doctor and the
Divorcé"), 28n2, 77n22;
Ore'ah nata lalun (*A Guest for
the Night*), 28n1, 78n28;

"Panim aherot"
("Metamorphosis"), 28n2;
"Shevu'at emunim"
("Betrothed"), 28n1; *Shira*,
28n1, 134-35n30; *Sipur pashut*
(*A Simple Story*), see under
Sipur pashut; *Tmol shilshom*
(*Only Yesterday*), 28n1, 29n10
"Agunot." *see* Agnon, Shmuel
Yosef: Works
Ahad ha-'Am. *See* Ginsberg, Asher
Akavia Mazal, 53-54, 57n26, 86,
104n4, 122, 123-24, 133n23,
134-35nn28-30
alienation: of Hirshl, 73; in modern
literature, 14, 25, 141
'Al kapot haman'ul (*On the
Handles of the Lock*), 28n2,
55n5, 57n26, 86, 105n11
allegory, x, 34n50, 133n20. *See
also* symbolism
Alter, Robert, 4-5, 29n12, 33n42,
34n56, 77n19, 104n2, 109n35,
133n20
anti-semitism, 3, 121, 129, 133-
34n24, 140, 144. *See also
Sipur pashut*, political reality
in
Anski, S. (Shloyme-Zanvl
Rapoport), 30n17
Appelfeld, Aharon, 136n39
archetype. *See* myth
Arnold Ziemlich, 42
Artz, Frederick, 30nn23-24
Austen, Jane, 6, 9-10, 28nn4-5,
30n16, 31n28

157

About the Author

Sharon M. Green has been teaching modern Jewish literature in the Jewish Studies Program at the University of Toronto since 1988. She earned a Ph.D. in Hebrew and Yiddish literature from the Department of Near Eastern and Judaic Studies at Brandeis University, where she was the recipient of numerous academic awards and fellowships. She has published articles on Hebrew and Yiddish writers in a diverse array of scholarly collections, and is currently at work on a new book on the relationship between literature and culture.

www.ingramcontent.com/pod-product-compliance
Lightning Source LLC
Chambersburg PA
CBHW030650110726
47901CB00002B/649